Praise for *Celtic Hedge Witchery*

"Joey Morris has worked tirelessly since 2013 to bring her incredible voice and passion to the witchcraft community at large. Hers is a rising presence that will enhance the chorus of Pagan voices for years to come."

—Amy Blackthorn, author of *Blackthorn's Book of Sacred Plant Magic* and *Blackthorn's Botanical Magic*

"*Celtic Hedge Witchery* is an invaluable tool for anyone wanting to deepen their connection not only to themselves but also to nature and the spirits that are all around. Joey Morris provides practical advice and techniques that offer a diverse and distinctive way of connecting to the three worlds that are associated with Celtic beliefs. The history, applications, and modern approaches in this book present old ways through new eyes and invite us all to look at the world differently, as well as our part in it. I highly recommend this book for anyone new to witchcraft or open to taking a different approach in their current practice. More than a practical guide, it is a way of being and highlights the importance of connection, protection, and honoring the world which we are and always will be part of."

—Jane Matthews, director of the World Divination Association

"Joey Morris has been developing her unique view on witchcraft and the Celtic path for years. Her deep devotion to her path and the spirits of the Celtic lands and Otherworld shines through in her work. Joey is a rising star in the Celtic witchcraft world, and I am excited to see her work birthed into the world."

—Annwyn Avalon, author of *Celtic Goddess Grimoire* and *Water Witchcraft*

CELTIC HEDGE WITCHERY

A Modern Approach

JOEY MORRIS

Foreword by Courtney Weber

WEISER BOOKS

This edition first published in 2025 by Weiser Books, an imprint of
Red Wheel/Weiser, LLC
With offices at:
65 Parker Street, Suite 7
Newburyport, MA 01950
www.redwheelweiser.com

Copyright © 2025 by Joey Morris
Foreword by Courtney Weber © 2025 by Red Wheel/Weiser, LLC

All rights reserved. No part of this publication may be reproduced or transmitted in any form or by any means, electronic or mechanical, including photocopying, recording, or by any information storage and retrieval system, nor used in any manner for purposes of training artificial intelligence (AI) technologies to generate text or imagery, including technologies that are capable of generating works in the same style or genre, without permission in writing from Red Wheel/Weiser, LLC. Reviewers may quote brief passages.

ISBN: 978-1-57863-867-3

Library of Congress Cataloging-in-Publication Data
Morris, Joey, 1985- author. | Weber, Courtney, writer of foreword.
Celtic hedge witchery—a modern approach / Joey Morris; foreword by
    Courtney Weber.
Newburyport, MA : Weiser Books, 2025. | Includes bibliographical references. |
    Summary: "This book delves into the secret liminal space exemplified by the
    English hedgerows and expands the reader's understanding of how to truly
    embody the witchcraft life, even for those who cannot visit an actual hedgerow.
    Readers learn how to connect to their natural witchcraft, find the sacred landscape
    within themselves, and commune with and benefit from working with spirits.
    Here is a revolutionary take on what it means to be a hedge witch in the modern
    era, one that shows the reader how to "come home" to both the Earth and to
    themselves"—Provided by publisher.
Identifiers: LCCN 2024042403 | ISBN 9781578638673 (trade paperback) | ISBN
    9781633413610 (ebook)
Subjects: LCSH: Witchcraft. | Magic, Celtic. | Nature—Miscellanea.
Classification: LCC BF1571 .M668 2025 | DDC 133.4/3—dc23/eng/20241121
LC record available at https://lccn.loc.gov/2024042403

Cover design by Sky Peck Design
Interior by Debby Dutton
Typeset in Adobe Garamond Pro

Printed in the United States of America
IBI
10 9 8 7 6 5 4 3 2 1

Celtic Hedge Witchery *is dedicated to Mama Lu, who took me under her wing and made me her spirit daughter—and changed my life for the better.*

CONTENTS

Acknowledgments	xi
Foreword by Courtney Weber	xiii
Introduction	1
A Note About Use of the Word "Celtic"	3
Hedge Witchcraft Theory for a Modern World	5
Theory of the Hedge, the Universe, and Everything	6
The Liminal Space	12
What Is Sacred?	13
What Is Intuition?	13
Why Use the Hermetic Principles?	14
Redefining the Hedge: The Spiritual Ecosystem	21
What Is Soul to a Hedge Witch?	25
Soul Rivers: The Flow of Awen	29
Defining the Hedge Witch	33
Spirit Worker	34
Shapeshifting and the Three Realms	37

What Is Celtic Witchcraft?	41
The Celtic Otherworld	45
The Three Celtic Realms	49
The Three Cauldrons	55
Cauldron of Wisdom	56
Cauldron of Motion	64
The Cauldron of Warming	74
The Sacred Grove	85
The Inner Sacred Grove	87
The Natural World as Spirit World	97
Earth Connection Activities	98
Spirit Offering to Nature	98
The Sacred Art of Wildcrafting	100
Hedge Witches and the Morrigan	103
Sovereignty and Celtic Mythology	103
The Goddess Morrigan: Shapeshifting	107
The Spirit Mask	113
Connecting with the Morrigan at the Hedgerow	115
Trees and Plant Spirits of the Hedgerow	119
Ogham as Gateways	121
The Spirit Tree that Connects All Spirits	125
An Exploration of Roots	127
Spirit of Silver Birch	128
Spirit of Hawthorn	135
Spirit of Rowan	141
Trees as Guardian Spirits	151
Non-Ogham Plant Spirits	152

Shadow Spirits of the Hedgerow	167
Healing Yourself, Healing the Spirits	168
Ancestral Spirits of Humankind	169
Working with Human Spirits	171
Animal Spirits When Shapeshifting	173
Visualization: Crow Spirit	175
Spirit Relationships in the Physical World: Sacred Space and Spirit Protection	177
Spirit Protection for Shapeshifting or Traveling through Realms	179
How to Shapeshift and Travel through the Other Worlds	183
The Art of Ecstatic Connection	183
Other Forms of Spiritual Ecstasy	189
The Shapeshifting Ritual Visualization	191
Conclusion	195
Notes	197
Bibliography	203

ACKNOWLEDGMENTS

Thank you to Judika Illes and the team at Red Wheel/Weiser for helping to make this dream come true. I appreciate them all so much.

FOREWORD

For many, the idea of something "Celtic" immediately evokes images: mists and mysteries, shimmering cauldrons, ladies in lakes, white-robed Druids, or other fantastical imaginings culled from Victorian-age imaginations and Hollywood films. In my own travels through the different Celtic modern worlds, a sense of that mystical spirit certainly exists, but what I have most appreciated about these dynamic, complex cultures is deeply grounded presence. This presence is often revealed through a gentle love and reverence for the green, the flowers, the bees and creatures of the wing, quiet symbiosis between human and animal, the people taking cues from the seasons and the cool, damp air. This spiritual approach reflects a relationship more than a taking, and one found in different flavors across the Celtic world, from Cornwall to Donegal and every other corner in between.

I'll admit, when I heard the title of this book, my mind immediately went to a few key lyrics from Led Zepplin's "Stairway to Heaven," a song that could be argued is enshrined with its own form of Celtic magick. The line I mention here references a hedgerow and the magickal secrets it holds. The hedgerow, something so commonplace, could easily be dismissed as just a fixture of the yard, and the uninformed might assume magick can only be found in the fantastical settings mentioned above. But both the band and the author of this marvelous book remind us that magick is found in the "ordinary." In fact, magick is found in every movement, breath, and blade of grass.

Author Joey Morris has consistently challenged common thought and unexamined approaches in modern Paganism. She is not afraid to call out extractive practices and call us in to build thoughtful ones. In *Celtic Hedge Witchery*, her beautiful work, Joey shares her deepest, most personal practices, gently nudging its readers to embrace and cherish a humble and accessible path, but one no less magickal than the famed stone circles of Britain.

Even more so, the exploration of the concept of boundaries symbolized by the hedgerow could not be more important than they are now. Boundaries are so often used to confuse and divide people, but Joey helps us understand that boundaries created by the hedge are more about exploring possibilities than limiting them, and more about unpacking possibilities than denying them. Through this supportive lens, the hedge provides a path more than a wall, one that encourages us to deepen our personal understandings of what a relationship with the natural world could be, and what kind of magick it could provide at such a pivotal time in human history.

For those who are curious, explore this book with the kind of wonder that certainly led Joey to write it. This work is not about recreating a tradition, abandoning one and reaching for another, but instead taking inspiration from this wonderfully diverse canon of mythology offered by the different Celtic cultures. There is wisdom in these stories, and there is wisdom in the natural world around us.

Joey's work is focused with modern practicality, but carries the gorgeous echoes of a past world, long loved and never forgotten, though perhaps misunderstood. She teaches us to take cues from the environment around us, no matter where we are in the world. It's not about trying to become something we're not, but instead to learn from this wealth of knowledge cultivated for thousands of years. *Celtic Hedge Witchery* offers the act of remembering, remembering where we came from and that these memories can be enshrined in the land on which we live, wherever that land may be.

Celtic Hedge Witchery is not a how-to-witch manual and shouldn't be treated as such. It's an invitation to open and explore parts of the soul and perhaps even a roadmap to approaching magick in a way that may be new to you. The greatest gift one could give themselves by exploring Joey's approach to Celtic hedge witchery is to become more aware of one's own approach. We are too quick to siphon ourselves off from our deepest, most innate spiritual impulses. This book invites us home and we are lucky to have it.

Of the many stories that the Celtic world offers, a recurring one is of sovereignty. Within the pages of *Celtic Hedge Witchery,* Joey Morris offers simple, gentle ways to connect with this very sovereignty, and goodness me, are we a people in need of it. From the very simple and powerful act of inhaling the breath of an herb to the deep transformational nature of soul journeys, Joey takes us there—or at least, opens the door in the hedgerow for us to find it ourselves.

Take your time with this journey, because, my friends, it will indeed be just that.

With every good wish,

Courtney Weber
August 2024

INTRODUCTION

If you have ever found yourself walking through a grove of trees and felt your entire world shift, then you might just have the stirrings of a witch within you.

The path of the modern witch is personal and diverse, for there are many ways to walk the crooked path, many labels that you may or may not decide to try out, until you find the pointy hat that seems to fit best. Or perhaps you will keep one in every color and embrace aspects of them all. Who knows? It is exciting to begin a journey of self-discovery and empowerment, and that is ultimately what witchcraft is about, as well as aligning yourself with the spirits that exist all around us in nature and beyond.

I do not believe you have to be born in Europe or have ancestry from there in order to feel called to what I have affectionately labeled Celtic witchcraft. I also believe you can practice hedge witchcraft even if you do not have access to the quintessentially European hedgerows.

While there are a plethora of books discussing Celtic mythology and folklore, I found myself wishing for a book that discussed what it means to be a Celtic witch in modern times. I love history—I even studied it at university!—but I have no desire to pretend that I live in any other time than now. The seeking for meaning—and of course, magic—in modern times was the driving factor behind *Celtic Hedge Witchery*. It is a search for *balance* (the word I use in spiritual discourse more than any other) between theory and practice in a world keen to venerate one or the other.

Witchcraft without knowledge is reckless, but witchcraft without heart is vivisection. It cannot be the divorce of mind and heart; it is a symphony of emotion and reason. Remove one, and there is no magic.

We shall listen out for the spirits whispering to us across the spiritual ecosystem, spinning tales of secret knowledge that humanity has forgotten. Our ancestors knew it. They harnessed this wisdom into power and magic, communing with the natural spirit world beyond this mortal curtain, communing with the plants and trees, setting fire to animal bones and divining the cracks, seeking to release themselves for a time from their human form and shapeshift into other creatures.

The modern world has sought to sanitize away the ancient magic, treating it with disdain, mocking it as primitive, or worse, trying to create a panic about the moral fiber of witches. So let us embody what it means to be a Celtic hedge witch, with our "other eyes" wide open!

We will get to know that spirits abound throughout this world: speaking largely from the shadows and revealing answers to the dedicated, guiding the curious along the narrow ridges of a spirit weaver's path, testing to see whether your courage fails you or your conditioning prevents you from reaching out for the wisdom that can be gleaned from the unseen mysteries.

These spirits take many forms; some shapeshift and bare their fangs, howling and hissing into the night, an open invitation to the seeker of bone-deep truths. They challenge us to fracture our human skeleton and let our spirit escape through the cracks, so we might see through their eyes, catching the scent of deepest soil and fragrant honeysuckle on the air, and sink our claws into a new measure of understanding.

To speak of spirits is to speak of death and dark spaces. We have sought hard as human beings to eradicate the truth of both, seeking to ignore that which causes us to fear. Death is hidden, dressed up, washed out, and put out of sight, the natural decaying process removed from thought and memory, and electricity rings out, polluting the night sky until we forget the beauty and simplicity of it.

To honor all spirits in life, and in death, is a magical act.

So too has humanity in general lost touch with the tools that support the artform of spiritual witchcraft, of hopping over the hedge and immersing ourselves in the wonder in nature.

Nature is neither dead nor unaware, and yet it's treated like a resource, something to be used. This rejection of nature is a deep rejection of what it really means to be human, part of an ecosystem that relies on every interwoven thread of energy.

We are meant to be the healers, guardians, and counselors of nature, not its destroyers.

The rise of the human tendency toward a dualistic mindset coupled with an unyielding stance of personal superiority has led the world in general to energetic stagnation. The idea that one person is right and another wrong and fixating on one's personal experiences as "all that is" can sway the magical practitioner away from the art of discovery and awe.

Let us discard the notion that there is merely one truth in this world and open ourselves up to limitless potential and possibility, for what we, as a collective, understand about the universe (and ourselves by extension) is constantly evolving.

The spirits reject constriction and dogmatic principle in favor of a crooked path, where the adventurous mind explores off the beaten track, where weeds and vines take back the route and their primordial souls can run, dance, sing, and howl.

And then so too shall we!

Amidst these pages we shall peer into the liminal spaces, call out to the spirits of the hedge, find the sacred groves that call to us, and weave together the magic between flesh and bone, crag and creek, Land, Sea, and Sky. We shall discover what it means to be a Celtic hedge witch in modern times.

A NOTE ABOUT USE OF THE WORD "CELTIC"

In the context of this book, "Celtic" is an umbrella term encompassing certain tribes in Europe that existed in pre-Roman times, spoke a variety of Celtic languages, and intermingled through migration, marriage, trade, warfare, and education. They may be traced through DNA lines or through archaeology that finds remnants of food or homewares at sites of interest, be they spiritual or trading. The modern concept of national borders did not exist for ancient people in the same way that we envisage them today.

I believe it is possible to balance a sense of national historical preservation in European countries without seeking to gatekeep spiritual practice through divisive tactics. Europe has been a melting pot of people, culture, and history throughout time—and not all of that history is pleasant to examine. There have been eradication and crimes against natives in other places in the world, and we should not seek to ignore that, nor should we ignore that much of the Celtic tradition, history, and stories have been lost to the romanization of Europe and the onset of Christianity.

I have encountered plenty who would seek to destroy my spiritual path because of my "heritage" even though they know nothing about it. I prefer to confine DNA to the interesting pages of history but not to create an environment of eugenic entitlement in the present. For my part, stories, as shaped by people, are far more interesting. My Welsh grandparents coming to England for an incredible opportunity in career, or my Irish great-grandparents coming to England to escape poverty. In their eyes, they traveled for love, for opportunity, and for a better life.

And so shall we, through the realms of spirit.

HEDGE WITCHCRAFT THEORY FOR A MODERN WORLD

A hedge witch is steeped in Otherness.
Standing on the boundary between seen and unseen,
Deep in conversation with spirits of tree, plant, and animal,
They seek out Otherness and travel between realms.

What is a hedge witch?

There are many definitions as to what makes a hedge witch, but for myself it means a witch who is a spirit worker, honors liminal spaces, and venerates nature. This comes from a belief that everything in nature has a spirit, and with practice, we can communicate with them.

The term "hedge" can have more than one meaning. In its literal sense, it is a border, usually between fields, that has been cocreated by humans and nature. Hedges are often comprised of trees or bushes (such as hawthorn) that have been grown into barriers. Hedges over time become ecosystems for birds, insects, and animals.

In an abstract sense, hedges are boundaries between our physical world and the world of spirits. By learning to cross the hedge, hedge witches seek to walk in other worlds.

THEORY OF THE HEDGE, THE UNIVERSE, AND EVERYTHING

To a Celtic hedge witch, certain concepts and ideas are the keys to the metaphysical locks of the practice of witchcraft. They are the foundation of many paths of witchcraft (not just this one), which can make knowing them super useful even if you decide to try a different witch hat on later.

Some of these, such as animism, are well documented, and you can find many detailed opinions from academics, historians, and witches alike. Some of these concepts, most notably the spiritual ecosystem and the inner sacred grove, are from my own personal gnosis. The concepts I have grown myself are rooted in the soil of academia and research, watered by the trial and error of personal experience, and grown with insight and intuition from a living, breathing spiritual practice.

While I have jokingly titled this section "The Theory of the Hedge, the Universe, and Everything," I want to assert that there is real wisdom in acknowledging the enormity of the universe and how little we actually know about it. I like to consider all the people I will never know or meet in my lifetime, going about their lives, laughing at jokes I may never hear, stressing about problems I will never know about. Or consider how little we know about our oceans. Or the thousands of books I will never get to read, or subjects that will forever remain alien to my mind in this incarnation.

Sometimes it is important, and humbling, to be in the realization of how small and uninformed we are—because arrogant hubris does more harm than good.

The Animistic World

Animism is the belief that everything has a spirit, an inner self, an essence of consciousness, and everything is connected through that spirit. This spirit is not simply self-contained but is also expansive, and within these pages the nexus (or center point) for the connections between all things, living and dead, are referred to as the *spiritual ecosystem.*

The lesson of spirits and how to work with them is integral to the path of the modern hedge witch, be this in literal witchcraft practice or symbolically in discovering and embracing common threads found in storytelling, in folklore, in mythology and history.

Working with spirits is a key component to witchcraft: to hear their wisdom, work alongside them for mutual benefit, and honor our interconnectedness. From there we can ritually seek out and connect to the power and knowledge hidden from sight, the mysteries that our ancestors knew. Animism is the conjoining thread that stitches all of this together.

The British author Emma Restall Orr describes animism thus: "Animism is a monist metaphysical stance, based upon the idea that mind and matter are not distinct and separate substances but an integrated reality rooted in nature."[1] This is the premise that the realm of spirit and energy behaves in much the same way as ecosystems in the physical and tangible realm, a suggestion that can be found in many interpretations of what laws govern our universe.

Some of the best known and most ancient are the Hermetic principles, such as the often-quoted Hermetic principle of correspondence, "As above, so below; as within, so without; as the universe, so the soul." You may have heard of this one before! It appears in many witch books, rituals, videos... it really resonates with the witch (and Pagan) communities generally.

We can theorize then that, as there is an interconnectedness between all living entities through their physical ecosystems (which can be identified and quantified in material and energetic terms), so too will those who have left behind their corporeal shell (yet are still sentient and exist within the realm of spirit) affect these ecosystems, as the soul and the universe are interlinked. The spiritual ecosystem would therefore be a reflection of the ecosystems in the physical world.

In the pursuit of magic for personal evolution and empowerment, most practitioners recommend considering the collective works of humankind, the wisdom within folklore, mythology, archetype, psychology, and so forth, most of which are the disciplines of the human mind. And yet it would seem prudent that while engaging in the process of magical ascent, all forms of intelligence should be considered, not just that immediately available within our minds.

Do not get me wrong, I highly recommend reading about these topics! But we are seeking *balance* as a Celtic hedge witch.

For generations, practitioners of the magical arts have sought out the counsel, wisdom, and knowledge of beings beyond themselves (spirits). Furthermore, in keeping with our focus on nonhuman intellect, many of those deities, allies, and spirits of all kinds have been said to appear in complete or partial animal or plant form.

The interconnected nature of nature being sacred to the ancients is wonderfully highlighted in "The Song of Amergin" from Ireland. It appears in the eleventh-century *Lebor Gabála Érenn* (Book of Invasions), a historical manuscript wherein divinity is described as a part of every part of nature. The ancient poem is somewhat of a mystery, with the author and date of origin unknown.

The following excerpt is taken from a version translated from Irish by scholar Lloyd Graham in *Echoes of Antiquity* as the early Irish "Song of Amergin."[2]

> I am a wind on the sea,
> I am a wave of the ocean,
> I am the roar of the sea,
> I am a bull of seven battles,
> I am a hawk on the cliff,
> I am a teardrop of sunlight,
> I am a gentle herb,
> I am a boar enraged,
> I am a salmon in a pool,
> I am a lake in a plain.

The idea that we are a part of nature, not separate from it, is a keystone to many different modalities of witchcraft, honoring every part of our world as sacred.

In a modern world that has disconnected us from nature, the reclaiming of this idea—and seeing how grounded in human history it is—can be a revelation. You may have already felt this connection as you stood in awe of a beautiful sunset or felt empathetically moved to protect the local wildlife.

I felt called to environmental issues aged six, and felt very cross that there was seemingly little I could do to help at that age! I signed up to the RSPCA magazine with my pocket money and supported the animals there nonetheless.

It's also a powerful reminder that we're not above nature but meant to be a part of it. The human narrative that we're at the top of the food chain is wildly inaccurate, and being connected helps us to see that this is hubris or a fear-based mechanism of control (or both).

You know the humorous version of the adage "What doesn't kill you makes you stronger. Except bears. Bears will kill you." It might be something to really think about! I like to consider just how terrifying the ocean is and how little we know about it. Get stuck in the middle of the ocean and chances of survival are not good, for all that people claim to be superior to nature.

The human physical body is also at a huge disadvantage to those within the animal and plant kingdom, whose evolution has adapted them to be superior in their environments. We as human beings may never fly unaided, but as witches, we may see through the eyes of a crow and allow our consciousness to soar. We may never shed our skin as a snake does, but we may learn the process through the connection to the energy of the serpent as to shed our metaphysical skin and ascend. We may commune with fungi and learn how roots commune between trees, or how plants have healed our bodies for generations.

Human beings have long sought to align themselves with the power of animals and plants, to embody their traits through the process of using totem and symbolism. We can attribute a family lineage with the symbol of the animal, such as was present in clans of people under an animal banner, and later through chivalry and family crests.

This still exists today with the idea of animals representing nations: the lion and rose of England, the bald eagle and oak of America, even the mythical unicorn of Scotland alongside the thistle, seeking to instill into people to a sense of national consciousness and connectedness under one banner.

This transcends everyday experience (as there are no wild lions anywhere to be found in England, for example), but it promotes a symbol, an idea, and an archetype to play on human emotional responses and evoke a sort of national pride through the prism of animal and plant imagery.

The lion, for instance, has been given names and titles by humans through which it has become associated with the hierarchy of power, namely through its designation as king. It has thus been attributed characteristics such as courageous, bold, and fierce, and in its place as a symbol of a country is supposed to embody and invoke those same qualities within the inhabitants.

So strong is the premise that it can be regularly found within promotional propaganda of advertisements, the wheel on which capitalism turns. As much of the mundane power in the world now rests in organizations and businesses, it seems that the influence of animal and plant imagery has shifted into their hands and is utilized to full effect. Pictures of cute animals have been selling items from toilet paper to insurance for decades, with the animals in question having little to nothing to do with the items themselves. Healing plants are often used to disguise items that are not healthy at all (a problematic process known as greenwashing).

This could be seen as a sort of bastardization of animal and plant spirit magic, depending on your personal ethical stance, although it does highlight the continued connection between the human mind and spirit to those in nature. It is interesting, then, that much psychological and philosophical debate attributes animalistic qualities to the so-called lesser aspects of our nature. This is yet another way in which humans seek to be above other souls—and thus another mode of thinking we need to unpick! We owe it to all the interconnected souls in the spiritual ecosystem to rethink this conditioning.

The philosophical work of Plato has provided the blueprint for much of the discussion around the human soul or psyche and has transcended into psychological analyses of the personality or self. In *The Republic*, he presents the notion of the immortal soul as suggested by Socrates as well as the notion of the tripartite soul, a soul divided into three distinct parts. The least evolved was the appetitive soul, located within the belly, driven by hunger and sexual desire; it is the part closest to the natural world (and clearly influenced Freud's animalistic "id" categorization of the personality).[3]

The three parts of the soul were considered separate, and the rational part of the soul (far more prized and exalted) was considered separate from the physical body altogether, located in the head. It is intriguing that as Plato refined his analogy, he turned again to animal symbology. In *Phaedrus*, the analogy for the tripartite soul is refined and presented as a charioteer struggling over a black horse and a white horse—an image, though completely problematic in its inferences, that has made its mark as an occult symbol through the evolution of the tarot.[4]

In seeking to distance the "higher" and more "evolved" part of the soul as the charioteer, Plato permanently linked the parts of the self to animal imagery, making the image timelessly famous, especially within spiritual circles familiar with tarot. These images even from time to time penetrate the popular marketplace through that old powerhouse of capitalism, leaving an impression on the general human consciousness. You can find images of tarot cards in music videos, fashion shows, and popping up in film or television media all the time.

By placing human value judgments onto the two horses, venerating the obedience of the white horse and demonizing the wild unbroken temperament of the black horse, Plato sought to lessen the desirability of these parts of the soul. As spiritual seekers, we shall not repeat old patterns that are problematic and the basis of racist ideologies, and instead seek all knowledge available to the human soul instead of cauterizing away important parts of the self.

As witches, we have to do away with separating the world of magic into black and white, which only reinforces the shadow within humanity that seeks to be dominate over others. If we are here to do the work that our soul calls us to do, we cannot hope to practice magic that gives breath to that work without the balance of all things, considering the heart and mind of both ourselves and all spirits that exist outside of the self.

As we go forward, we shall be considering many of the animal and plant spirits commonly associated with mainly European witchcraft, particularly hedge witchcraft—the types of animals considered familiars or spirit allies to magical practitioners throughout history—and theorize about how the mostly European Celtic mythology (influenced heavily at times by Greek mythology, which is sometimes considered the "gateway" to Europe if not a part of it) and folklore give hints to the deeper lessons these spirits can teach us in a modern age.

As with all matters of spirituality, the lessons within provide a guide and do not exclude the differences that come with personal experience and perception. Your magic and awareness are built on your life choices and how you have interacted with the world around you. The essence of a spirit has commonalities to all humans, whether that be accepted through the history of teaching it to be so, from the spirit itself, or by the propaganda that arises from human fearmongering, such as in the case of snake energy.

What is also true is that you can integrate your own personal gnosis balanced with the wealth of stories behind the energy of a spirit. To question is wise; to rebel is necessary. This is the magic of wildness and the primal: it does not comply with expectations.

THE LIMINAL SPACE

What is a liminal space, and why does it matter to a modern Celtic hedge witch?

The liminal is balance incarnate. A place between, it is both the boundary and the crossing of it, a threshold, a place that is betwixt and between, saturated with magic and mystery, a physical location that thrums with etheric presence. It may cross into different spirit realms and be a connection point between them.

It is sacred.

As we reach outside of ourselves, our spiritual tendrils stretch out into the spiritual ecosystem; we seek understanding to the mysteries of the universe. We "tap in" to an energy that is expansive, sometimes confusing, and more than slightly Other.

The liminal spaces are places of limitless potential and possibility, the deep breath before the plunge, the expansive darkness in the mind before thought, the endless choices found at the crossroads.

Liminal is a space within a space that is part of the Otherworld, something beyond our physical senses, felt with the heart and seen with psychic vision. It is the supernatural ability of bilocation, being in two places at once.

It is worth noting that we, as human beings, can deconstruct everything into nothingness, build something from the smallest electrical impulse of inspiration, and change the course of history on a whim.

This is interaction with the liminal.

Human beings may not always do this for our highest good, however. We categorize every part of our existence, clutching desperately at this sense of importance and immortality. It screams "we were here, we existed, we mattered" for all future generations to witness and remember.

The spiritual ecosystem—that which connects all liminal spaces—remembers everything. It is my belief that memory is the currency of life force. It is a human fear to be forgotten, but in the spirit world, nothing ever truly is forgotten.

Boundaries are liminal spaces. They are the crossroads, the intersections, often between where energetic ley lines are said to cross. Here ley lines are meant to be given as pathways of the spiritual ecosystem, which are made up of energy and cross over one another at different points in the realm of spirit.

WHAT IS SACRED?

As we are going to be discussing the idea of the sacred quite a bit from here on out, it is probably best to explore what we mean by that. The Cambridge Dictionary defines *sacred* as "considered to be holy and deserving respect, especially because of a connection with a god."[5]

Sacred is simply a word to describe human reverence for a place or person, based on agreed-upon ideals, usually of Otherness. It is a human contract with a place, an acknowledgement, an intuitive feeling that certain places in our world spark a feeling of reverence. This means to be enchanted by them, to sense the old magic inherent in a space, or feel the spirits that reside there.

This connection is facilitated once again by the spiritual ecosystem that feeds and relays soul messages across all the realms of existence. This is experienced as intuition, in dream states, or a gravity of emotional feeling that is sometimes beyond description.

Sacred is a description for soul memory recognizing liminal space.

When seeking to understand the mysteries behind witchcraft, I feel there is a balance between intuition and the universal laws that have been created from the logical, rational self. When it comes to hedge witchcraft, intuitive communication is an integral part of the overall spiritual practice. This will be part of the foundation of learning to communicate with plant and spirit allies and travel across different liminal spaces (into spirit realms).

To engage in the practice of spirit communication and spirit travel—two key components of modern hedge witchcraft—we need to understand as much as we can about how our minds connect to other realms and some of the laws of the universe that facilitate interspirit travel. It is finding that balance once again between intuition and practice.

WHAT IS INTUITION?

The Merriam-Webster Dictionary definition of *intuition* is as follows:

1 a: the power or faculty of attaining to direct knowledge or cognition without evident rational thought and inference
 b: immediate apprehension or cognition
 c: knowledge or conviction gained by intuition
2: quick and ready insight[6]

To intuit is a practice that is difficult to explain but widely understood. It is akin to when someone asks how you know you are in love—you simply know.

When it comes to spirit communication, traveling between spiritual realms of existence, or interpreting our experiences, intuition plays a major role because the communication usually occurs outside of regular or mundane channels, which can lead many people to doubt their experiences. Without a tangible physical reaction or data to reassure us, many of us wonder whether or not an experience is "real." Here we are doubting the liminal spaces because they rely on extrasensory perception (psychic skills).

I personally feel that applying the Hermetic principles of the universe can be helpful here, even though they are not Celtic in origin. This is an integration of modern knowledge to deepen our current understanding of the world—much like not rejecting scientific discovery because we are on a spiritual path.

This is adaptive practice—applying reasonable spiritual theory when we find ourselves bereft of the Celtic versions from history due to the purging of much Pagan practice at the hands of the Christian church.

WHY USE THE HERMETIC PRINCIPLES?

To the best of my knowledge, there are no "Celtic universal laws" in terms of explaining the governing laws of the universe and how to work with them. Modern Druidic orders often take tenets from ancient Breton laws, but these are more about legal governorship than spiritual laws, which are then applied to personal behavior.

There is a great deal of information about cosmological setup, some of which we will be examining, detailed descriptions of the Otherworld, animism, the power of inspiration, poetry.

Ultimately we are utilizing an ancient system that began in Egypt after Alexander the Great's conquest in 332 BCE and has been evolving ever since. We know that the ancient Celtic people were absorbed largely into the Roman Empire, which would begin the erosion of their culture and religious practices as Christianity sought to replace them. Ancient Hermeticism spread across the West, and many forms of modern spirituality have been influenced by the 1912 occult text *The Kybalion*, which introduced the seven principles of Hermetic thought. Several of these cross over into magical theory, such as the aforementioned "as above, so below," which is the principle of correspondence.

The Principle of Correspondence

> As above, so below; as below, so above. As within, so without; as without, so within. This Principle embodies the truth that there is always a Correspondence between the laws and phenomena of the various planes of Being and Life.[7]

Intuition is implicit within the principle of correspondence. It is the vehicle through which we travel to other planes of existence. It is an inner knowledge that we cannot fully explain that comes from being connected to everything else in existence. It is hearing or feeling that connection.

It is one of the ideas that help to explain the spiritual ecosystem, that as everything in our physical plane is constructed into ecosystems that directly impact the life force of all within it, so is this true in the Otherworld (other realms of existence).

It also can be helpful in intuitive hedge witchcraft when we consider correspondences of energetic vibration of, say, plants. Human beings have learned to ascribe medicinal and spiritual meaning to plants that have been learned over time, documented, tested through trial and error, and then generally accepted by the collective to be correct. That well-known aspect of a plant within herbalism may actually be telling of a plant's spirit nature.

I have come to understand that plants and trees (as well as all other forms of life) tend to have both singular energies and personalities and are connected to the "All" form of their type, which forms a central hub or nexus for all spirits of that type to connect to.

So, for example, there is an "All" consciousness of dandelions that one can tap into that connects all dandelions, which links their commonalities. This is where I believe the common threads or correspondences come from—as learned by witches over the centuries.

This forms a web of information shared by plant spirit and human spirit alike through many different mediums: spiritual contact, constant use over time, reaffirming of these ideas by spiritual practice, the passing of information through books, etc.

The idea of blowing on a dandelion to grant a wish is so entrenched in folklore that it bypasses one heritage and is an incredibly common experience connected to childhood worldwide (at least, to all climates in which dandelion grows). This is incredibly useful to the spirit of the dandelion, ensuring the continuation of its heritage, and is deeply rooted in the human experience of childlike wonder that it connects us back to a state of believing, which is crucial for magical practice.

As hedge witches, this principle can assist in spirit work and spirit travel, which tends to be subdivided into *hedge-riding* or *shapeshifting*. All of these experiences are in the magical portfolio of the hedge witch, seeking to discover as much as they can about the world of spirits, and so having an understanding of the principle behind spirit work is essential.

We can also see a reflection of this idea within the "Song of Amergin" in which the poet sees himself within every aspect of nature with the statement "I am . . ." As witches, we know ourselves to be a part of nature, not separate from it. Witchcraft is a natural art that stems from this connection.

The Principle of Mentalism

The all is mind; the universe is mental.

> In a certain sense, the Universe is itself a living mind; one that is connected to all other minds. As such, every action you take and every thought you take is an interaction between different aspects of the mental.[8]

This principle highlights the importance and power of our mind, something which is the foundation of much of our spell casting within witchcraft. It is also relevant to my personal understanding of the universe as a spiritual ecosystem, which I have, at many points in my journey, compared to the neural network of the human mind.

The human mind is defined as the activity of the physical brain, neurons firing within it creating reactions that we perceive and are very real to us but completely (at least currently) singular in the experience. We cannot show someone else our memory as we experience it. We can relate it to them, create something physical or vibrational to pass along a message of it, but that is the limit of how we can express it.

Intuition, then, is a "gut feeling" actually located within the liminal space between the conscious and subconscious mind. The brain-gut, if you will! This can be tapped into by the consciousness of other spirits, other minds, within the spiritual ecosystem—and thinking that plants or animals can't have as high a level of consciousness in the ether as humans is simply human hubris.

The connection of all living spirits (and those in other planes of existence) through the principle that we are all one living mind (the universe experiencing itself) is a common thread in witchcraft studies.

I will add that from my personal gnosis, I believe that memory is the currency of life force, the point and purpose of our lives. We feed memories back to our original soul or self (which is akin to the All-spirit of the dandelion I mentioned earlier, only it is our own version), so that we experience multiple lives, realities, and planes of existence simultaneously.

When we sleep, we may dream of other realities, other lives, other times in history which feel so vivid and real that we cannot shake the feeling we've glimpsed into another part of ourselves. I believe that is the case—that memory being sent back to our "original self" has got crossed over and we've tapped into it.

Many witches engage in past-life recall or seeking memories from alternate lifetimes to enrich their knowledge of their soul, and I believe this principle can assist in that process.

The Principle of Vibration

Nothing rests; everything moves; everything vibrates.

Vibration is the key to attuning to and feeling the energy of different spirits within the spiritual ecosystem. Everything in the universe vibrates, albeit it at different frequencies, different rates. The only difference between all manifestations of consciousness or mind—be it matter, thought, emotion, thing, or circumstance—is their corresponding rate of vibration.

The higher the rate, the less dense (or more subtle, or less physical) that thing is.

The lower the rate of vibration, the more dense or physical the thing is.

Everything we experience in our world is conveyed to our brains through vibration, and the interpretation or perception of our brains is why we experience things as solid. Therefore this law supports the existence of other realms of reality, it is just that our brain is not naturally conditioned to receiving their vibrations in order to perceive them.

As hedge witches, we can utilize a number of methods in order to change our vibration and assist us in visiting the other realms: meditation, dance, eating or imbibing certain plants (such as mugwort tea), smoke or incense rituals, drumming, singing, and so forth. We do this in order to spirit travel or shapeshift to commune with other spirits, to meet them at their vibration.

To continue with the dandelion analogy, a singular dandelion will have its own personality and vibration but will also vibrate with the energy of the "All" of dandelions.

I find that as humans we might intuitively ascribe feelings, colors, ideas, and emotions to each particular energy and then seek to explain these to others, which is why, for example, we attribute the dandelion's energies to Jupiter and the element of Air.

One magical property of dandelion is given as divination, especially spiritual messages—likely at least one thread of this knowledge being tied up in the idea of blowing on a dandelion to make a wish to influence the future. Thus we come to understand something about the energetic vibration of dandelion as it has impacted on us as a species.

If we seek to meet the dandelion spirit on its vibration, then we have to match (or at least seek out) its frequency.

The Principle of Rhythm

Everything flows, out and in; everything has its tides;
all things rise and fall.

There is a pattern to the changes we experience.
Everything goes through cycles that move from birth
to death and then rebirth. *This Principle applies just as
much to the Earth's seasons as it does to our bodies.*[9]

For intuitive hedge witchcraft the idea of our experiences changing and shifting in rhythm with the earth is helpful to connecting to the messages of the other spirits who are governed by and, in their physical incarnation, live by these cycles.

That is to say that their messages, their medicine, and their magic can change depending on what the season is, where in their life cycle they are, and their current biological mission—whether to grow, to spread seeds, or to die off and decompose.

The Principle of Cause and Effect

Every cause has its effect; Every effect has its cause.

There are two primary ways that causality can affect intuitive hedge witchcraft: the effect that human action as a collective has on the understanding and energy of spirits, and the changes to the understanding of a particular spirit based on our own personal actions and interpretations.

Human collective behavior can often be negative, and as such has a major destructive impact on the spirits of the ecosystem.

Would dandelion always have been as rebellious an energy as it is without human beings designating it a pest and trying to eradicate it? I suspect that the history of the spirit of dandelion has been shaped by the essence of resistance. Dandelion will happily work with witches and those who recognize its brilliance and worth, and pay it the proper respect, which is not always the case with other spirits.

I have encountered tree spirits that are enraged, and disrespected land spirits can cause human beings all sorts of problems. This is a direct consequence of ignoring the spirits of other creatures because they do not behave the same way as humans in their sentience.

Assuming that we, as witches, on a personal level seek to be understanding and respectful of the other spirits, our understanding of their energy is still impacted by our personal choices and actions. Choice is a cascade of energy that begins with intuition combined with personal desire that is a powerful display of magic and personal power all by itself.

We may feel drawn to a particular plant, tree, or animal, and cultivate a spiritual relationship with that energy on purpose. We have chosen to exalt that particular energy and seek it out, for reasons of our own—preferences, relevant memories, personal agendas or necessities—and that impacts on our interpretation of the energy we intuit.

All of these elements must be remembered when we connect with and seek to understand a spirit that is other to us. They are not us, and yet we interpret them through our particular lens. This is not a universal spiritual truth—it is our truth, a half-truth.

(I will not be including the Principle of Gender for spirits because I feel it is important to move outside of this when engaging with them).

Hopefully through the laws of Hermeticism we can begin to understand our intuition and its role in connecting with the spiritual energies of other spirits—a relationship with whom helps our magic, our understanding of the world, and, as such, of ourselves. Though it is not Celtic in origin, it certainly gives us a solid foundation in universal law that can be applied to theories of the universe and other realms that we do have from Celtic tradition and folklore.

REDEFINING THE HEDGE: THE SPIRITUAL ECOSYSTEM

The spiritual ecosystem as I understand it is a mixture of reasoning using universal laws and spiritual experience (or UPG—unverified personal gnosis).

Visually—that is, within spiritual meditation—it presents itself as an intricate root system with a bioluminescent glow, a complex weaving of spirit threads that are both alive and sentient and yet a part of a larger cognizance. I see reflections of it within nature all the time, both within ourselves—our neural networks or vascular system—and within nature, such as the underground network system that connects tree roots and fungi.

I particularly like the words of the French philosopher Lucien Lévy-Bruhl as a summary of the interconnected nature of our universe and how it is sacred:

> A sacred spot never presents itself to the mind in isolation. It is always part of a complexus of things which include plant or animals species which flourish there at various seasons, as well as the mythical heroes who lived, roamed or created something there and who are embodied in the very soil, the ceremonies which take place there from time to time, and all the emotions aroused by the whole.[10]

This analogy gives us an idea as to how memory is interwoven into the fabric of a place, even though those who originally performed the acts of heroism or performed rituals have returned to the world of spirit (or perhaps incarnated elsewhere).

Ecosystem exists in everything: the outer world, the inner world inside of us, and in the Otherworld of spirit.

We are all connected.

This is true in the physical world in which all plants and animals share the same DNA, built from the same amino acids, with the majority of plants and animals having their genes in common.[11] And as it is in the physical, so it is within the spiritual. The spiritual ecosystem is the connection between each and every ecosystem in our reality, visualized in a thousand different ways (which hinges on the perception of the individual connecting with it).

For myself it is energetic roots or threads that glow with a kind of spirit version of bioluminescence, viewable only with our "other eyes" (or our psychic senses) in the meditative process of journey work.

Our entire world is made up of ecosystems that are all interlinked and interdependent on one another. To take away a single living part of an ecosystem results either in its extinction and the deaths of all other parts of it, or a radical alteration of that ecosystem so that the previous arrangement no longer exists.

If we took away all life on this planet, then would the spiritual ecosystem cease to exist? I believe that to be the case. Without the balance between the realms, between the parts of soul incarnating and those at rest in the spiritual realms, there would be nothing to experience, no new memories to be made. The entire system would collapse.

As modern hedge witches, we can connect to this idea very easily through the experiencing of nature through physical hedges first, which are major hubs of life in Europe. Hedgerows in the physical world often have unique ecosystems that support biodiversity in the wild: "Almost all our native mammals have been recorded as being supported by hedgerows, which are home to over 500 plant species, 60 species of nesting bird and many hundreds of invertebrates."[12]

The hedgerow is a physical boundary as well as a liminal space, which showcases the harmony that can be achieved when man and nature work together. It is not the destruction of nature, but the evolution of a healthier relationship wherein animals and plant life can grow and adapt. Nature is incredibly adaptable, a quality we should seek to reflect in ourselves as witches.

It is thought that hedgerows in some form have been around since the Bronze Age, and it is my feeling that they represent some of the last remnants of our ancient woodlands that have long since disappeared. Hedgerows represent history and memory of the land on which they were built and from the spirits they were built by and from: "Our old hedgerows can still map the lines of feudal boundaries, reflect the social and political changes the country has lived through, retain the floral fingerprint of the lands they were cut from, and collate the signatures of agricultural change."[13]

The trees chosen for their adaptability and protective nature have been woven into the hedge and cultivated. Yet the ancient woodlands have been destroyed in our physical realm only. Their spiritual blueprint still exists in the spiritual ecosystem, and the spirits of the plants, trees, and animals remember.

I personally feel the loss of the ancient woodlands in my soul much as I mourn the loss of the great library of Alexandria; much wisdom has been displaced from our physical realm to the stampede of so-called progress. Together we can walk through the spirit realm woodlands, find the ancient groves still in the spiritual ecosystem—but imagine what it must have been like for the ancestors who revered, respected, and even feared the ancient woodland!

The physical hedgerows are a ghost of what used to exist in the physical world, but their energy in the spirit realm is still connected to the ancient woodland spirits. Hedgerows are gateways, doorways, a place where we can feel the humming of memory just out of sight, a place where we can connect into if we do the work of the hedge witch that opens us up to this experience.

We are meant to be connected with the natural world, far more so than we are today. I believe that a lot of the emotional and soul disconnect we feel in modern times is a direct result of this disconnect. Nature has become somewhere we "go to" rather than something we are an integrated part of.

Currently there are those in our world who are trying to suggest our future is not biological but technological, so that we become integrated with a false ecosystem that tricks our brain into believing we are living when instead we're simply plugged into artificial intelligence (AI). I find this ridiculous and full of hubris—just an excuse to go on destroying the world and seeking to subvert the consequences.

It will be humans who are destroyed if we carry on—the earth will survive without us.

Respecting bodily autonomy begins with the earth—she is living, breathing, feeling. She is a spirit, and the connection point between all other spirit realms made manifest. A nexus of life force. We don't own her, but we do owe her—everything.

The borders of our skin are akin to hedgerows. Our skin is the border within which everything is contained. The same can be said for our auric body on the spiritual level. If we choose a spiritual path that aligns ourselves with accountability in our personal choices and honoring the sacred within ourselves, we begin to heal our bodies and our connection with the earth body.

The artificial technological world cannot replace this. We emulate these energetic ecology blueprints when creating matrixes for creative invention (such as the aforementioned AI). The digital landscapes we have fashioned are based entirely on the natural ones—a pale imitation that is lacking the soul of the spirit-rich ecosystems we live within and that live within us.

And the soul remembers.

The spiritual ecosystem is that blueprint in the spirit realm, something human beings have been aware of for generations. You are the container for the most intense form of sacred energy. You are the embodiment of the sacred, a vessel for your soul, infused into your bones and marrow with stardust and earth, and through the connection of the physical and spiritual, you connect with the Divine.

The boundaries of your body are just like the hedgerows within modern hedge witchcraft—by growing your psychic senses, you can hop over those boundaries into the spirit realms. Your body is a work in progress between nature and humanity, and it connects you to all the spaces outside of yourself.

You are a living breathing hedgerow, a sacred grove, a human, and a spirit. A vessel of the spiritual ecosystem. An ecosystem within yourself, and a part of a great many ecosystems without yourself.

And with practice and openness, you can be a hedge witch too.

WHAT IS SOUL TO A HEDGE WITCH?

I always smile to myself when trying to define the unknowable mysteries, because it feels like herding cats. I think the wisest answer is this: no one truly knows the full extent of what the soul is or what it means to have one. Philosophy throughout human history has been devoted to the pursuit of this knowledge, for better or worse, and if humans are adept at anything, it is disagreeing with one another. This is undoubtedly the case when people are arguing about spirituality—something steeped in mystery and dependent on the entirely mutable perception of humankind.

My Theories of Original Soul and Multiple Incarnation Existence

I will say, before giving my thoughts on what a soul might be and why we might incarnate on this planet as part of a soul journey, that this is largely what the Pagan community has come to describe as "unverified personal gnosis" (UPG). I find the idea a little peculiar given that all resources on spirituality, such as myths or stories from folklore, were created by humans at some point in history, and apparently only when it has been around long enough to be widely disseminated and agreed upon does it become a kind of accepted and unified gnosis.

This does hint at the interconnected nature of the human experience, that people value the collective over the personal when it comes to knowledge. It's a slippery path, though, which has some pretty nasty side effects when left unchecked. The problems of divisive rhetoric are meant to harm and silence others—usually, in my opinion, for money. This is just to say that all opinions and experiences are valid, it just doesn't make them more valid than anyone else's.

This being said, the following describes how I feel the soul operates, based on over twenty years of experience, experimentation, journey work, and soul searching. I will give the broad overview of soul experience first and tie this into Celtic witchcraft specifically once we have discussed these key concepts.

The Original Soul/Self and Parallel Existence

To engage with being a witch is to seek information, especially about the mysteries of the unknown, to better understand our souls and our place in the world.

I am sometimes overwhelmed by the amount of information available on this earth that I will never know, the people I will never meet in this lifetime, and all the places I couldn't possibly visit in one lifetime. This feeling, being in awe of the immense nature of experiences available, leads me to feel that we cannot possibly accomplish real understanding in one lifetime. Therefore we likely have a kind of mission statement for each lifetime, as our soul reincarnates into different bodies, different time periods, perhaps even different realities.

I feel that there is the original soul (or original self) outside of this bodily incarnation that exists within the spiritual ecosystem, and a small part of that soul (which is always connected to the whole through the network of spiritual energy) incarnates into each body. The information we collect in each lifetime (our memories) are fed back to the original soul through soul threads (visualized as roots), which is the nexus for all the experiences we have received this far.

This is the function of the spiritual ecosystem, to connect all original souls to their incarnations and feed memory into the spiritual ecosystem.

We are all the universe experiencing itself.

Each lifetime is rich with information, experience, thought, and emotion, which add to our collective soul knowledge. I believe this is also where feelings of déjà vu (the feeling that one has lived through the present situation before) and incredibly vivid dreams of alternate lifetimes come from: when memories in the soul threads cross over and we receive information from other parts of our overall soul experience.

This is also a method that can be practiced and tapped into to retrieve this information—a version of what some people refer to as the Akashic records (a compendium of all universal events, thoughts, words, emotions, and intent ever to have occurred in the past, present, or future in terms of all entities and life-forms, not just human).

I personally feel we are living out multiple lifetimes at once, and time is not linear in the way that human beings often perpetuate it to be. Time is our construct, our way of making order out of chaos, to give our lives structure. It is also based on our observations of the earth, and the universe is far more expansive than the conditions found on simply one planet. Therefore "past lives" is a bit of a misnomer, as we might be living out a lifetime in a different era concurrently to this one—which may explain a deep yearning for a different way of life or time period if the original soul is particularly enjoying that experience.

I also distinguish between the etheric body and the auric body when examining the idea of our spirit body and how to work with it to further our psychic abilities—particularly for our purposes of connecting and communing with nature spirits.

- Etheric body: The blueprint of our spirit body as we incarnate into this world, given from the original soul. Unaltered and unaffected by our experiences. Most connected to the mission or soul work of this lifetime. Some call it the higher self.
- Auric body: Our aura being, influenced by the actual experiences of our lifetime, our physical body and state, affected by our emotional, physical, and mental health, as well as memories.

Soul Missions and the Etheric Body

I feel that we innately know who we were before we were conditioned by the world. That innate knowing is our intuition again, our witch sense. The following activity is greatly beneficial when seeking to uncover what your intuition is trying to tell you about your soul mission in this lifetime. I advise this journal exercise to begin the process of uncovering the blueprint of your etheric soul:

1. Draw two stick figures next to each other to represent you, divided by a dotted line.
2. Label one figure "Original me" and the other "How I am now."

It is usually easiest to start with the "How I am now" section because people find it easier to criticize themselves. Technically this exercise is not about that criticism, but rather objectively seeing the ways in which you have altered yourself (emotionally, mentally, physically) for outside approval, because of societal or cultural pressure, for work, and so on.

These will likely feel like necessary alterations at the very least, but can easily be burdens, shadow-wounds (more on this later), and inauthentic parts of the self.

Remember, there is no shame here, we are just observing the parts of self that do not feel "real" or "how we really want to be." These are the blockages to our soul purpose, and we feel them as such.

Make notes on how this feels and manifests in each area of your life. You might start with only a few notes and come back to this exercise once a month.

On the other side, consider how you were as a young child or when you last felt really free. This is allowing your intuition to remember the parts of yourself that you incarnated with into this lifetime, the blueprint for who you are and what you came here to do.

It is helpful to reconnect with this version of yourself if you are feeling lost or disempowered by the world, which can happen regularly.

A great draw to the path of witchcraft in general is the autonomy it provides, because there is no one path, there is no rule book (no matter how much some people try to claim there is). Witchcraft is the art of energetic change, to enforce one's will (spirit) into the physical world, and an empowered self leads to greater results with manifestation.

Self-Soul-Creation

Once we have begun steps to identify our authentic etheric self at a soul level, we can begin balancing that with the soul work of this incarnation. The act of self-soul-creation is the realization that, at any stage, you can make the choice and proactive steps to change who you are and your life. You are not stuck.

Many things in life promote the idea that we cannot or should not seek to change our circumstances, and social conditioning encourages this. It wants you to get stuck in a pattern that keeps the status quo in society—benefiting the selfish elite over the ecosystem. Have you noticed most of us in later life never try anything new until we absolutely must? Humans are almost hardwired to avoid change because we equate it with danger (mostly subconsciously).

We visualize ourselves as rocks instead of rivers, and the Celtic witch within points to all the parts of us that are rivers: we are beings made of water, we need the rivers of water and air to survive. We break everything down into rivers of blood within us to be absorbed, and rivers flow through our every system. We cry, we sweat, we spit, we urinate. Biologically we are designed to heal and overcome, although we become less efficient as we age—that is due to our returning to be a part of the earth and the spiritual ecosystem.

I believe the process of self-soul-creation starts with unpicking the conditioning, and continues with the process of creating, which we can begin to understand by tracing the etymology of the word itself:

> create (v.)
> "to bring into being," early 15c., from Latin *creatus*, past participle of *creare* "to make, bring forth, produce, procreate, beget, cause," related to Ceres and to *crescere* "arise, be born, increase, grow," from PIE root *ker- (2) "to grow." De Vaan writes that the original meaning of *creare* "was 'to make grow,' which can still be found in older texts."[14]

Etymology is fascinating because it traces the root of a word through language back through time. It is almost like the memory within language! This gives us an inkling of what the nexus of its soul memory means.

So, the process of creating *is* the process of self-growth, and once you give yourself permission to become whoever it is *you* want to be, you break down the first wall. The process of unpicking the conditioning and personal creation will be ongoing and cyclic—they will work in tandem and will oppose one another at points.

SOUL RIVERS: THE FLOW OF AWEN

Creativity and creation are soul rivers that flow into us from our original self and through the divine spark in the spiritual ecosystem. They are what nourishes our soul, what we love, instead of what we "ought" to love or have been told to love. Sometimes, it is not the thing we are the most naturally talented at—perhaps we have carried this gift, this ability, from another lifetime, and so it comes easily to us. But perhaps there is limited joy for us in carrying on with this because it is already conquered, known, or just simply doesn't pique our excitement any longer.

We are meant to be adventurous as human beings. We are meant to get a flutter of uncertainty and wonder as we step outside our comfort zones, and fully engage in the acts of creativity that we love to do.

The conditioning of the world says it is only "worth" something if you can "sell" it to other people—one of the saddest problems of our time is how capitalism destroys the soul in favor of survivability. So many people trade away their happiness so that they can manage through life. The system is rigged against us. We have to find inventive ways around it, incorporate our creative loves, and express who we truly are in this life.

We can find a career in what we love, as long as we have strong boundaries with it, as long as we take the time to be creative, inventive, and find the silver lining in all things. When people say they "hate" a particular element of their work, I suggest finding an alternative perspective. Find a way to be creative with it—I tell stories in newsletters, share experiences in reviews, and share love in my adverts. This will look different for everyone—perhaps singing as you travel, or adding a gratitude list to your to-do list. (The only one I can't get around is taxes, so I guess we invest in decent coffee and make our way through it!)

Sometimes we must go back to the keywords of who we want to be and why. The dream—if it is worth it—will always sustain you through the roughest patches of shadow work. Keep a diary, a mood board, a journal, of who you want to create within your life. Consider it fluid—you are always adjusting it, adding to it, going back to it as a well of inspiration.

In the Welsh, Cornish, and Breton Celtic traditions, the flow of inspiration that is divinely led is known as Awen. For a definition of Awen I shall refer here to the one being used publicly by the British Druid Order:

> The quest for Awen is a quest for the spirit of Druidry itself, and, as such, it brings together many paths. We may pursue the quest as historian, linguist, poet, philosopher, priest, magician, shaman, and in many other guises. Each, in its own way, helps us to gain understanding. . . .
>
> The first recorded reference to Awen occurs in Nennius' *Historia Brittonum*, a Latin text of circa 796 CE, based on earlier writings by the Welsh monk, Gildas. After referring to King Ida of Northumbria, who reigned from 547 to 559, Nennius says that: "Then Talhearn Tad Awen won renown in poetry."[15]

As with all definitions of something in spirituality, with Awen we have varying accounts. It is claimed that the word itself predates Christianity and snuck its way into the poems and stories that were handed down, thus being a remnant of Paganism. There are various definitions of the word itself, translated as inspiration, muse, genius, or poetic frenzy—which might be a reference to Celtic spells that were often uttered in one breath. This could also be supported by the etymology of Awen having the Indo-European root *-uel,* meaning "to blow."

What is certain is the widespread nature of the concept, which appears in the *White Book of Rhydderch,* the *Red Book of Hergest,* the *Black Book of Caermarthen,* and most prominently in the *Llyfr Taliesin* (Book of Taliesin), which draws parallels between the spirit world and the concept of Awen.

As far as I can tell, recent dictionaries simply give the descriptor of "poetic inspiration" when it comes to describing what Awen means. In my mind, Awen is a gift of insight, encouragement, knowledge from other incarnations, and inspiration from the original soul and the spiritual ecosystem.

The modern symbol of Awen is three lines descending from three dots, which is most famously found in Charlotte Guest's translation of *The Mabinogion,* the most well-known text of Welsh Celtic mythology and folklore.

In the Welsh bardic tradition, it is intrinsic to the legends of the goddess Cerridwen, created by her in a cauldron and intended to bestow her son with otherworldly talent and knowledge, but the young man Gwion inherits it instead when the cauldron overboils from inattention.

The myth reads as a mystery tale, with deeper meaning behind it than is first presented. Before Gwion can receive the otherworldly gifts, he is forced by Cerridwen to shapeshift through different animal guises and flee through each of the Celtic realms of Land, Sea, and Sky, which we will explore regarding their relevance to Celtic hedge witchcraft. He becomes one with animal spirits and the spirits of the elemental realms before he is reborn as Taliesin, the greatest bard who ever lived. To shift outside of one's confinement is to engage with the liminal spaces. It is to walk, run, fly, or swim, across the hedge and back.

Awen and soul creation are important concepts because they show the meshing of intentional creation and divine inspiration . . . and what is the essence of the hedge if not this?

The physical hedgerow, a whisper of the edges of the once wild woodlands, is now a cultivated created boundary line with its own adaptive ecosystem. It showcases what can happen when mankind and nature coexist. The hedgerow in spirit is a liminal space, the gateway to the ethereal sacred groves, a crossroads to the realm of nature spirits and their wisdom.

Poetry and groves and rules are all sacred, and this is because all of these are tied together, a sacred bond between the realm of the living and the Otherworld. It all moves through the land, and we are bonded to the earth in our physical bodies. As hedge witches, we shall journey to glimpse these connections and learn from their mysteries.

DEFINING THE HEDGE WITCH

When it comes to defining what a hedge witch was, or is generally considered to be today, the information can be quite convoluted and mixes elements of general witchcraft definitions with Wiccan aspects thrown in.

Similar themes suggest that hedge witches tend to be solitary, involved in herbalism of some sort, perhaps hearth witchery (or kitchen witchery), must be near a physical hedgerow, and celebrate the wheel of the year (the modern Wiccan version). All of these may well be true to your personal practice. While hedge witchcraft will certainly align with many other types of witchcraft—particularly green witchcraft, which connects with and uses plants and herbs—it feels as though many definitions are lacking in the soul of what it means to be a hedge witch.

The best example in my opinion comes from the wondrous Rae Beth in her book *The Green Hedge Witch*:

> The Hedge witch of old, the Hagazissa, worked to keep the balance between the human community and "wild spirit," by which was meant the domain of nature spirits, elves, place spirits, elementals and all kinds of natural untamed forces. . . . In today's world, with humanity so much in control (and so little at peace) . . . the situation is rather different. So we often need to reinterpret old traditions and magical practices in the light of our knowledge that much wilderness (the domain of wild spirit) has been destroyed or is under threat.[16]

Within this definition there is the memory of what the hedge witch perhaps once was, although there may be some romanticism involved. Witches throughout history were not often perceived in a favorable way, and accusations of witchcraft could easily ruin or end a person's life. When we step into the role of a modern hedge witch, we acquire some of the weight of legacy that history has created around the title. Good and bad and all the shades in between. What does it mean to embody the essence of being a witch so completely, with every fiber of your being?

The knowledge that this world is a complex system of Otherness and interconnected tendrils of energy that go unseen and largely rejected by the masses is a grave and burdensome responsibility that weighs heavily on the mind of many a witch. The history of so many lives lost and the worrying modern narrative of hatred that falls from many lips brainwashed by patriarchal religion is no small thing. But year after year people go out into the woods looking to find themselves, feeling bereft of connection and seeking something magical.

The call is within their bones—your bones—something that might not entirely make sense, but your intuition is whispering that this modern life is not what was promised. The knowledge that the earth needs us to step up and take care of her—and ourselves, really—and that extends to all the spirits in this world.

This is my definition of what it means to be a modern Celtic hedge witch: it is a calling to be a guardian—not quite like the Hagazissa of old, but instead to honor the interconnected nature of the ecosystems of earth and spirit. To learn to travel through the realms, learning the mysteries from the past but also from the present. To seek to embody change in a world that desperately needs it, bringing balance and living in harmony with nature, with the cycles of ourselves and the world.

To not fear Otherness, but to embody it.

The hedge is not only a physical location but a spiritual one, and working with spirits is a large part of what it means to me to be a hedge witch.

SPIRIT WORKER

A hedge witch is one who works with spirits. A hedge witch is aware that the natural world is not quiet. It is always humming, always singing, with spirit voices that go unheard by the majority of people, for they have forgotten how to listen. The disconnection from and apathy toward the ecosystems of the earth and beyond is a soul sickness of the modern world.

We live in a world of spirits.

To commune with spirits is, in my opinion, the beating heart of Otherness at the center of witchcraft. It shadows my every step as I walk the path of the hedge, knowing that everything in this life has a spirit, and those spirits do not stop existing once one earthly incarnation is complete.

Hedge witches are the embodiment of the liminal space between life and death. Our memories matter, and within them we carry the imprint of all those who have gone before us. We are sacred messengers, and we can both hear what once was and speak into being what shall be.

Spirits are more than death echoes, they are sentient, connected to the whole in the spiritual ecosystem, be they human, plant, animal, or other. They communicate, relay information, teach and guide us, and impart their memory—individual or from the collective—so that we might be more in tune with the overall ecosystem.

A large part of my witchcraft practice has been learning how to listen to them, understand different forms of communication, and understand what my place is within the ecosystem—a place that continuously grows and evolves.

Knowing the world of spirits is, at this point in our evolution, a matter of intuition and experience over one sole soul methodology. There is no one way to commune with spirits.

It has been my experience that spirits exist both in the individual and in the collective. This is similar to understanding the psychology of human beings, how we consider ourselves both an individual and a part of the whole. Science fiction has been devoted to the issues of valuing a whole—even a hive mind—over the individual, and in nature, hive minds do exist. It is my belief that the spirit realm is more expansive and complex than this, allowing for a collective ecosystem of memory to exist concurrently to individual spirits with their own personalities and agendas.

This allows for a collective memory of each species which I refer to as the "All" spirit of any genus, as well as individual spirits with their distinct personalities and character traits. This is as true for trees and plants as it is for humans and animals, if one knows how to communicate with, and connect to, their spirit.

Every incarnation of every type of spirit is adding to their collective All experience.

Some spirits live far, far longer than we do, such as tree spirits. I feel that so many witches are drawn to trees because they represent a physical reminder of longevity—of all the memories beneath their bark—and their spirits guard all of the realms (and connect them).

We sense this with our psychic abilities.

Hedge witches seek to learn the different languages in the world around us. To be a hedge witch is to be an "earth-based psychopomp" working with all of the spirits of nature. The definition from the Oxford English Dictionary of what a psychopomp is as follows:

> One who conducts souls to the other world after death, a function ascribed in Greek mythology to Hermes. In analytical psychology, the word used by Carl Gustav Jung (1875–1961) to describe the role of the anima and animus (3) as go-betweens, linking the ego and the unconscious (2). psychopomps or psychopompoi pl. [From Greek *psyche* a soul + *pompos* a guide, from *pompein* to send or conduct].[17]

I also quite enjoyed the examples of psychopomp as given by the Collins Dictionary due to a certain fox spirit reference:

> "A psychopomp is a guide, an intermediary, between the living and the dead." *Sunday Times* (2009)
> "The tracks are of a fox, the psychopomp of his first, lonely month exploring the edge-land." *Times Literary Supplement* (2015)[18]

There are a number of things to unpack from these definitions that help us to understand what a hedge witch is. The first and most basic understanding is one who communes with (or directs) spirits, which is something many modern witches partake in. There is a rich history, in fact, of spirit communication and witchcraft.

The second is that being a hedge witch can often mean being of service to the natural world, to both commune with and on behalf of spirits. This can be to act as a guardian to a place, protecting a physical ecosystem and the spirits that reside there, to learn knowledge from spirits to deepen your knowledge of the world around us, or to seek purpose in life through this communication. For some, it is the confirmation of their psychic gifts from which there was no escape and left them feeling peculiar. It gives a personal direction to those who previously felt lost.

Spirits can act as guardians as well as guides, assisting us when traveling through the other realms of existence. The hedge witch is one who seeks to journey to other planes of existence and explore the Other realms.

SHAPESHIFTING AND THE THREE REALMS

In hedge witchcraft, there tend to be two versions of the spiritual journeying and/or spirit work known as shapeshifting. The first version is when part of the witch's soul purposefully splits from their body and transforms into (usually) an animal shape and travels through the Other realms.

The other form of shapeshifting is "riding" along with the spirit of an animal (oddly enough, very close to what Terry Pratchett described in his *Witches Discworld* series!).

When a hedge witch travels, they seek to find other realms of existence. There is a general agreement that there are three main spirit realms, based on European folklore and mythology, which crosses over at several points with Celtic cosmology and Irish mythology (though the creation of a cohesive path or system from this information is more UPG than it is reconstructionism). I am not particularly interested in trying to strictly reassemble the past; instead I am interested in what I have experienced as a witch to be true, and above all, what works.

The truth of the landscape of the Otherworld is this: no one really knows, and personal perspective will always be different.

It seems reasonable to me that, from all stories and accounts we have from others, be it in folklore, stories, or tales from other witches, that the realms themselves may shapeshift. It is up for debate whether the other realms are shapeshifting because that is their nature or because they are so complex and vast that they cannot be understood by the limitations of our human minds and so appear to be shapeshifting to us.

In the practice of shapeshifting, there are three main realms: the lower realm/world, the middle realm/world, and the upper realm/world, all of which are connected via the axis mundi (or the spirit tree of the universe). How these realms are viewed seems to depend on the recounting of the individual witch or practitioner relating back their experiences.

The lower realm (sometimes seen as the Underworld) is one associated with the element of Water, or the Celtic realm of Sea, and is ruled by the Moon. In visiting it, it often appears dark, and we find our senses particularly alert to both danger and experience within it. I personally experience it as a labyrinth or night garden or as caves by the sea.

This is the realm more frequented by witches, perhaps because of our general love for the night and the cycles of the moon. It is associated with Otherness, our ancestral line, memory, the subconscious and dreaming, the dead, and, of course, shapeshifting.

In much of Celtic mythology, the sea was considered the realm of the dead as well as the physical location where entrances to the Otherworld could most easily be located—such as islands surrounded by water or caves where earth meets water. One of the reasons this could be the most frequented realm for shapeshifting by witches is that it is connected to the dream state, where many travel outside of their body without full awareness of having done so. It is connected to the most primal, animalistic, and intuitive part of the soul, which would most easily lend itself into shifting into an animal form. The ideal state for out-of-body experiences is said to be between sleeping and waking.

I associate the Celtic realm of Sea with the Cauldron of Warming, located in the lower stomach.

As the three realms are connected by a central pillar, the axis mundi, so too are the three cauldrons connected within our bodies, our inner spiritual ecosystem, with our spine being a perfect physical symbol for the tree of life.

The act of shapeshifting is considered an advanced technique that requires spiritual protection, with several safeguards being put in place before one even attempts it. These include:

- Being in a sound mental and emotional state in waking life
- Performing personal cleansing and grounding techniques
- Having cleansed and repaired any auric damage
- Having contacted protector spirits to guide you
- Wearing protective amulets, charms, sigils, or jewelry
- Having a spiritual anchor in place to bring you back to the waking world in a hurry if your spirit feels in danger

We will examine these in more depth in the chapter on protection and spirit work, as well as the process by which to engage with shapeshifting and realm travel, after we have formed relationships to the spirits who will assist and protect us while doing so.

We access other realms of existence by altering our conscious state through acts such as meditation, trance, dance, drumming, singing, or substances that alter our state of mind. By doing this, we are tapping into the spiritual connection "as within" so that we might astral travel "so without."

When journeying to the lower realm, the witch may travel downward through the Cauldron of Warming, through blood and water, traveling down the axis mundi through the sea or other body of water.

The upper realm is the polar opposite of the lower and is traveled to in an upward motion along the axis mundi as well as within the body, therefore being connected to the Cauldron of Wisdom (within the head) and the realm of Sky.

In psychology, this would be connected to the superconscious, the ethical center, which is the logical, rational part of the self. I would also connect it to the concept of divine inspiration—that is Awen in the Welsh Celtic tradition.

As Awen is considered the driving force behind a person's actions in life, this is the realm most connected to the ideals of self, structuring, archetypes, and manifestation in the physical sense. It has an energy of creation and destruction that favors the warrior archetype but can be used by healers.

When visiting the realm, it seems to be created out of light and heat, which is often blinding and uncomfortable. It has a "kingdom of the skies" feel to it, but it seems to be the least traveled (or discussed) realm by witches—perhaps because we tend to favor the moon, or perhaps because it has an echo of a Christo-Heaven idea to it.

The middle realm is connected to the realm of Land or Earth, represented by the Cauldron of Motion at our heart. It is our world but "peeled back," so that we perceive it with our Other eyes or psychic senses. This would be the world as it is if we were free of our conditioning, if our energy vibrated to be perceptive, if we were not so bogged down by the daily grind.

It is considered to be the most dangerous realm to shapeshift through, as many spirits wander here freely and have easier access to you as it is closer in proximity and energy to us. Thus, spirit attachments or harm are more likely occurrences for the unprotected or unprepared, as one of the dangers of shapeshifting is that you run into spirits who will deceive you or cause you harm. Not all spirits are benevolent, and many do not care for humans. There is also an element of false security when traveling through the middle realm because it feels less alien, and therefore we let our guards down.

The idea that a sacred tree is at the center of these realms is a common spiritual motif that can be found across Celtic traditions as well. In the Irish tradition, for example, there is the *bile*, a sacred tree found at the center of chieftain and sacred ceremonies as well as the five founding trees of Ireland referenced in the *Dindshenchas* as "legendary guardians of five Irish provinces."

> The five most sacred trees of mythology and legend: *Eó Mughna* (an oak which bore acorns, apples and nuts), *Eó Rossa,* "the tree of Ross" (a yew), *Bile Tortan,* "Tortu's tree" (an ash), *Craeb Daithi,* "the branch of Dath-I" (also an ash), and *Bile* or *Craeb Uisnig* (another ash) had stood at the centre of five provinces.[19]

The tree being of central importance to the gathering of chieftains and for spiritual ceremonies is widely agreed upon by historians. There is also surviving evidence that such trees were connected to the Otherworld, such as in this example from "The Sick-bed of Cuchulain":

There is a tree at the door of the court;
It cannot be matched in harmony;
A tree of silver upon which the sun shines.
Like unto gold is its splendid lustre.[20]

Entrances to the Otherworld were found in liminal sites, often where land met water, such as in caverns with rivers or islands, in burial mounds, beneath lakes, and so on. It is no coincidence that these entranceways were liminal and found where the different realms (Land, Sea, and Sky) converged, and thus that we utilize our inner connection to these realms to travel through the spirit world.

WHAT IS CELTIC WITCHCRAFT?

A generalized definition of what Celtic witchcraft entails might be "the modern practice of witchcraft that draws on Celtic roots, a form of Paganism that is influenced by Celtic folklore and mythology."

The Oxford English Dictionary defines *Celtic* as "Relating to the Celts or their languages, which constitute a branch of the Indo-European family and include Irish, Scottish Gaelic, Welsh, Breton, Manx, Cornish, and several extinct pre-Roman languages such as Gaulish."[21] People get very argumentative when it comes to definitions, with the need to separate out reconstructionism and neo-Paganism, or seeking to orchestrate who is "allowed" to call themselves Celtic (or not), and this can devolve into comparing family trees or accidents of birth in terms of location ... the list goes on.

I believe in the evolution of witchcraft.

Witchcraft is never going to be a cookie-cutter practice. It speaks to the soul of the individual, whipping up their excitement, their desire for adventure. Their soul becomes ignited in the quest for personal transformation.

Witchcraft is an enigma, arguably beyond being fully comprehensible to human minds. Every time a definition arises to cage it, witchcraft shapeshifts, drops the skin of the outmoded, carrying with it tradition but not being chained by it.

Witchcraft is a survivor, because berated, bullied, belittled, or burned at the stake, witchcraft lives on.

I define my personal path as Celtic simply because it draws from the history and mythology of Celtic people and deities. I prefer the umbrella term rather than seeking to limit a magical practice further by identifying it as from a certain country or read out every location my ancestors lived in Europe to justify my deeply soul-connected beliefs.

I honestly feel that arguing about Celtic roots detracts from real conversations about racism and cultural appropriation of marginalized people (which are needed and necessary in modern Pagan circles). It is worth noting, though, that the term *Celtic* is very broad and, as already shown, applies to several different groups of people from various countries who have their own beliefs and cultural norms.

Much of what we know about these people are from secondhand sources with a Christianized agenda, as most ancient Celtic people had an oral tradition and thus did not believe in writing down their sacred mysteries:

> Celtic scholars do not doubt that there was an active oral narrative tradition functioning in pre-Christian and medieval Christian Irish society. Until recently, tradition-bearers with amazingly large story-repertoires could be found among Gaelic-speaking peasants and fishermen in Ireland and Scotland.[22]

History is never an exact science, as what we know about it is informed by bias: the bias of the individual documenting a source, or the person discovering, cataloguing, and interpreting it. I have always seen history as another form of storytelling, where we seek to understand where we come from. This is another subject that is devoted to the eternal question "Who am I?" although it often seeks to address "Who are we as a result of who they were?"

I have a deep love of history, but I am certain that the stories that are woven by ancient people (as well as the stories we weave about them) are always a sort-of truth, with embellishment, agendas, and mistranslations being rife. History is often about making a sense between the lines, knowing that educated informed guesses are the best methodology and that theories are being suggested, accepted, and disproved over time. There is no permanent constant in history.

Only mathematicians and Sith deal in absolutes.

The main tenet I will give for following a Celtic path is . . . respect.

Research what history and folklore you can, do not make claims for the Celtic people based on wishful thinking, and do not claim there is only one form of Celtic belief (because the variation across Europe has been and still is vast). Know that we do not live as our ancestors might have lived—and to try and do that is not the point. We were incarnated into this vessel, in this lifetime, to learn the spirit lessons of this life. Our experiences are vital to our original soul.

Celtic hedge witchcraft merges what I have learned about hedge witchcraft, the liminal spaces, the spiritual ecosystem, and being influenced by elements of Celtic mythology and folklore. I am influenced deeply by my connection to the goddess Morrigan, who is a complex deity, being a shapeshifter in all things. In the surviving mythology, she is shown to literally shift her shape as well as reshape the social and political landscape of Ireland via warfare and as a goddess of the land and thus sovereignty.

There is not one god or goddess of the hedge, nor of Celtic witchcraft, because the practice is diverse and personal. But the Morrigan is my goddess, and thus influences my perspective. The connection to the Celtic realms of Land, Sea, and Sky have been deeply moving when in sacred ritual space. But above all, it was my personal spiritual calling, and perhaps yours too—and nothing and no one should be allowed to take that from you.

THE CELTIC OTHERWORLD

What is the spirit realm in a broader sense? Is it the same as the Celtic notion of the Otherworld?

Author Sharon Paice MacLeod in her discussion of the Celtic structure of the universe puts it thus: "From the evidence we have, it appears that the Celtic Otherworld (or worlds) were conceived of as existing nearby (and parallel to) our own plane of existence. . . . aspects of the Otherworld mirror those of the mortal realm, yet in many ways it was considered superior to our world."[23]

This is how I too feel about the spirit world—that it is just beyond our mortal sight, viewable in glimpses when we connect with our Otherness, or in dreams when the scales slip and we walk unbound by earthly restriction, though I differentiate by seeing the triad of other realms.

The spirit realms are beautiful and terrifying, but above all they themselves are a shapeshifter—an energy that reacts to the consciousnesses within it, a reflection of their memories, which are infused into the spiritual ecosystem, and perhaps their expectations too.

The energy is impacted by the spirits, for they are a part of the spirit world just as the spirit world is a part of them. The connection is more tangible and yet less solid; it mutates and flows and changes in the blink of an eye.

The three different main realms are impacted by the kinds of spirits that reside there—creating a symbiotic relationship in those spirit ecosystems. They are a reflection of our world as it is, as it has been, and as it could be. Stories play out across its landscape, remembering all that has long been forgotten by humankind, infused with living expression of emotion and thought.

It is every story ever told of a strange unknowable world whose rules make no sense (if they exist at all) and that divides itself over and over into ever-expanding pockets of universal spirit. What you see in the spirit world will change depending on who and where you are in your spiritual journey, and likely it will impress further change upon you too. Change is the universal constant, after all.

There are many varying stories of the idea of a Celtic Otherworld from different cultures that present a similar narrative. The Irish name for the Otherworld is Tír na nÓg, meaning the land of eternal youth, with the most thorough description found in the tale of Oisín and Niamh of the Golden Hair, which is almost an Irish equivalent to the Welsh tale of Rhiannon. Like Rhiannon, Niamh is a woman of otherworldly beauty in search of a husband while on horseback. Oisin, who is out hunting deer, accepts her proposal, and the two of them leave for Tír na nÓg, as the magical steed ferries them across the ocean to the Otherworld.

A beautiful world awaits Oisin, which grants his every wish just from his thoughts, but it is flawed in that the land does not allow for failure or disappointment, and without these, Oisin finds himself bored, wishing for danger or real combat.

> Oisín begged Niamh to let him return to Ireland, but she was reluctant. Although Oisín thought that only a few years had passed, it had been 300 years back in Ireland, since, in the land of Tír Na nÓg, time slowed down.
>
> Eventually, Niamh saw how much Oisín missed his family. She agreed to let him return to Ireland to see them again. "Take my magical white horse," she told him. "Do not get off this horse, and do not let your feet touch the ground, or else you will never be able to return to Tír Na nÓg again."[24]

Naturally he fails, falls to the ground, ages three hundred years and dies, but only after imparting his tale.

In Welsh stories, the Otherworld is called Annwn or Annwfn, with various tales suggesting it has different parts to its realm. The following is from *The Mabinogion* (the main Welsh book of folktales) relating to Pwyll, who has an encounter out hunting with a lord of Annwyn, Arawn:

"Chieftain, if I've committed an offence, I will redeem your friendship."

"In what form will you redeem it?"

"As appropriate to your rank—I don't know who you are . . ."

"A crowned king am I in the land I am from."

"Lord," said Pwyll, "good day to you. Which land is it that you are from?"

"From Annwfn. Arawn king of Annwfn am I."

"Lord, how might I obtain your friendship?"

"This is how you might obtain it: there is a man whose kingdom borders on my kingdom, who is constantly at war with me. He is Hafgan king of Annwfn. The removal of this oppression from me—which you can do easily—will win you my friendship."[25]

Pwyll appears later in *The Mabinogion* when he chases after an otherworldly maiden on horseback and wins her hand in marriage. This is the beginning of the mythology around the goddess Rhiannon, and at this stage in the tale at least, it mirrors Niamh and Oisín.

The Gaulish Celtic belief in the Otherworld is likely the basis for the hedge witch belief in the three realms: "To the ancient Gauls, the spirit realm was both a terrestrial location and a spiritual one. . . . they also maintained a belief that there were three realms: Albios, translated roughly as the upper world . . . Bitu, the land/the world where we live; and Dubnos, the underworld."[26]

So what do we, as modern hedge witches, make of the spirit realms, the Otherworld?

We begin with the narrative from our ancestors, while understanding that we only have a fraction of their belief system left, a kernel of mystic truth nestled in unreliable authors, Christianized doctrine, and a dearth of original material. We can glean from the tales that the Otherworld is simply that: Other. It is like our world but not. Time moves differently there, and it is full of spirits, information, magic, and danger. Nothing might be what it seems, and our regular senses cannot be trusted. Indeed they might work against us as we long for our own reality if we linger too long.

It is beautiful, enchanting, designed to appeal to our senses, with its own rules and rulers. It is a place we have limited knowledge of even if we study folklore and what our ancestors wrote about it. Each journey might reveal some new truth to you, some new visage, a different perception of magic, the world, the universe. The evolution of rules in a place where time moves so quickly can only be guessed at!

It can be exciting, and it can be dangerous. Before we venture into the realms, we must know how to protect ourselves, and then build up relationships with spirits who will guard, guide, and assist us. Only then may we walk into the unseen realms—albeit it with the upmost respect.

The greatest of spirits are the gods whose stories interweave with the Otherworlds, and there are many whose protection, wisdom, and very nature align with the journeys we might take. For myself, the goddess who called was (and is) the Morrigan.

THE THREE CELTIC REALMS

It is generally agreed that the ancient Celtic notion of cosmology was divided into our world and the world of the gods (the Otherworld), and within our world there were three realms of existence: Land, Sea, and Sky.

The more I practice witchcraft, the more attached I feel to the concept of Land, Sea, and Sky. This trinity reflects the sacredness of the natural world to which I feel a deep connection, and the three cauldrons connect us to the inner realms of Land, Sea, and Sky, as we shall see.

Entrances to the Otherworld in Celtic mythology "were most often said to be located in or underneath hills, beneath lakes or under the sea, on islands situated in lakes or off the coast, or in halls or buildings encountered by chance in the night which disappear with the dawn."[27] This is also true for many mythological adventures in other cultures.

In his definitive works Liam Mac Mathúna, Professor Emeritus of Irish at University College Dublin, discusses at length native Celtic beliefs in the ordering of the cosmos, referencing stories from the surviving mythology. He suggests that the father of Cú Chulainn shows the connection between how the universe was structured (and is potentially falling apart) and his son fighting: "In *The Book of Leinster* . . . Súaltaim employed them at the start of the episode in order to express the awesome extent of the tragedy which was threatening his son, Cú Chulainn, implying that it was equal in significance to the destruction of the natural order of the universe."[28]

This can be found in the Irish mythological epic the *Táin Bó Cúalnge*:

In nem maides ná in muir thráges ná in talam condascara ná inn é búadrugud mo meic-sea so ac comrac ra écomlund for Táin Bó Cúalnge?

    Is it the sky that breaks or the sea that ebbs or the earth that quakes or is this the distress of my son fighting against odds on the Foray of Cúalnge?[29]

The realms of the cosmology can also be seen in the Welsh text *The Mabinogion* and the tale of the birth of Taliesin, the greatest bard to have ever lived. In this tale, a young man named Gwion is tasked by the goddess Cerridwen to stir her cauldron of Awen, a magical brew that contains all the knowledge and inspiration in the world, meant to be a gift for her own son, Morvran, who was born cursed.

Depending on the retelling, Gwion either takes the brew for himself on purpose or by accident, and then faces the wrath of the goddess, who chases him and forces him to shapeshift into different animals:

    [He] changed himself into a hare and fled. But she changed herself into a greyhound and turned him. And he ran towards a river, and became a fish. And she in the form of an otter-bitch chased him under the water, until he was fain to turn himself into a bird of the air. She, as a hawk, followed him and gave him no rest in the sky. And just as she was about to stoop upon him, and he was in fear of death, he espied a heap of winnowed wheat on the floor of a barn, and he dropped among the wheat, and turned himself into one of the grains. Then she transformed herself into a high-crested black hen, and went to the wheat and scratched it with her feet, and found him out and swallowed him.[30]

Both stories from different regional Celtic mythologies highlight the importance of Land, Sea, and Sky to the Celtic people, as both highlight the established triune of existence, which if destroyed, would cause the cataclysmic destruction of our reality.

In the tale of Taliesin, the young boy Gwion is initiated into the sacred mysteries and is forced to shed his skin and shift into animal form and travel through each of the realms until he dies and is reborn through the sacred cauldron (womb) of the goddess Cerridwen. When he is reborn as Taliesin, he becomes the most famous bard ever known (Merlin from the King Arthur tales, although "Merlin" was technically his title, not his name). After shedding his skin, traversing through the realms, and being reborn, he becomes beloved by the mystical force of Awen—more connected to the rivers of souls than any before him.

The Celtic importance of a triune—of the number three—is a well-documented phenomena within the folklore and modern spiritual practices alike. Many of the ancient deities had a triple aspect, including the Morrigan (whom we will be discussing later) in her forms of Morrigan, Macha, and Badb (sometimes given as Anu, Macha, and Badb). The shamrock has three leaves, and there are three cauldrons of the soul from the Irish poem "Cauldrons of Poesy" from the seventh century. The sacred triskele symbol, the earliest creation of which is dated to the Neolithic era, has three legs as can be seen at the entrance of Newgrange in Ireland. The symbol is thought to represent the triads in existence, the inner and outer worlds, life, death, and rebirth, as well as the unity of the mental, physical, and spiritual self.

The journey of the modern Celtic hedge witch is a journey of soul learning through the Otherworld, and as the liminal spaces of hedgerows exist within the physical world, so too do they exist in the Otherworld.

As we consider each component of what makes up that Otherworld and its sacred triple nature, we can better connect to the world of spirits who inhabit it. If each of the legs of the triskele represent one third of existence, then the center could be seen to be the symbolic gateway to the Otherworld, which forms a downward triangle. The symbolism in esoteric communities for a downward triangle varies, but it often thought to symbolize the divine feminine, a cauldron, or represent "so below" and "so within" from the principle of correspondence.

The sacred grove has been my most frequent and profound visualization of inner sacred space and represents an inner connection to the ecology of the ancient forests. That is what lies behind the gateway at the center of the self when journeying as a Celtic hedge witch: a place where all spirits are honored, a place between our world and the Otherworld, where we can commune with deity. The hedgerow forms the lines of the triangle, and thus becomes a border to the spirit woodlands as once it was on earth.

Because there are always three pathways, it stands to reason that within each of the realms of existence there are doorways that open to the Otherworld. We can connect through Land, or Sky, or Sea. The hedge witch walks the road of Land, while still honoring and communing with the spirits of Sea and Sky. We are never truly separate from any of the triune, because all are necessary for existence, but we may favor one method to gaining entrance.

Hedge witches work with the art of witchcraft that overlaps with green witchcraft, the spirit connection to and the magical practices with elements of the land, such as herbalism, tree magic, activism protecting nature, the alchemy of natural ingredients. It is not that we cannot connect through the gateways of Sea and Sky—and at some stages in our practice we should engage in that practice to balance our experiences—the memories and knowledge we send back to our original soul. Like Gwion in his spiritual metamorphosis, our soul seeks the balance of three, to know our place in each of the realms before we can be reborn. Life is the constant cycling through of stages of being, of emotions, of shadow, and of self.

We will find later when connecting to animal spirits in the spiritual ecosystem that we will naturally gravitate toward one from each realm. It is also completely possible to gain spiritual connection at other points of earth, such as within barrows, ancient structures of memorial built as burial mounds. We can always see the reflection of the hedge energy in such places, however—manmade structures that both serve a physical purpose and create a boundary to the spirit world.

When we come across natural formations that also serve this purpose, we are likely in for a far wilder and stranger trip to the beyond, which is perhaps why humans are still wary of mushroom circles!

Before we examine how to connect through the hedgerow, we should first examine the triad nature of our own soul through the Cauldrons of Poesy, so that we can understand that we too are connected in the energy of three. This will enable us to deepen our understanding of and connection to the spiritual ecosystem, seeing ourselves as a reflection of it.

- Land: The realm of experience. The teacher. The earth on which we walk and feel everything, as our ancestors did before us. The realm of choice and manifestation.

- Sea: The healer. All rivers return to the sea, and so we all flow back to the spirit realm. Our memories flow like rivers guiding us through life and beyond. Emotion and memory held in the water.
- Sky: The messenger. All that is communicated travels through breath, whether it be heard out loud or simply with the heart. Through its vibration, poetry is made possible.

THE THREE CAULDRONS

We have already mentioned the three cauldrons as being energetic centers within the body that correlate to the three realms of Land, Sea, and Sky, as well as the three realms of upper, middle, and lower. The three cauldrons are a Druidic alternative to energy centers within the body. This is a system based on an extensive seventh-century medieval Irish poetic text, *The Cauldron of Poesy*:

> My true Cauldron of Incubation (warming)
> It has been taken by the gods from the mysteries of the elemental
>   abyss
> A fitting decision that ennobles one from one's center . . .
> the making of fearful poetry,
> vast, mighty draughts of death-spells. . . .
>
> I sing of the Cauldron of Wisdom
> which bestows the merit of every art,
> through which treasure increases,
> which magnifies every common artisan,
> which builds up a person through their gift.
>
> I sing of the Cauldron of Motion
> understanding grace,

accumulating knowledge,
streaming poetic inspiration as milk from the breast,
it is the tide-water point of knowledge,
good is the dwelling of speech.[31]

The poem itself is a good deal longer, but this sample highlights the main spiritual purpose of each cauldron within the self. The cauldrons are each connected to a part of the self, mainly the head, the heart, and the stomach.

The cauldron is a fascinating tool that carries weighted symbolism both in folklore and in modern witchcraft practice. The cauldron is present in so much of Celtic mythology: Cerridwen's cauldron is infamous, and the Welsh god Bran has a magical cauldron that can reanimate the dead, which in the tale "Branwen ferch Llŷr" he gives to his sister's husband the Irish King Matholwch. The Dagda in Irish mythology is said to have a cauldron that satisfies his guests' hunger no matter what, and in the medieval poem "Preideu Annwfn," penned by Taliesin, King Arthur is said to go to the Otherworld in hope of acquiring a magical cauldron.

The religious and spiritual significance of the cauldron is sprinkled throughout Celtic literature, with the *Cauldron of Poesy* poem linking it to the triple nature of the human soul.

CAULDRON OF WISDOM

The Cauldron of Wisdom is linked to our highest spiritual and artistic selves, connected to the mental self and the inspiration that comes from the spiritual ecosystem, Awen. On one leg of the triskele, this cauldron is linked to the realm of Sky, and in the shapeshifting realms this would be the upper realm—which makes sense as it is within the head (thus the highest point within the body).

The Cauldron of Wisdom is also related to dreaming, which is widely considered to be a spiritual act, for when we are sleeping it is as though we are bearing witness to a theater of the imagination. The realm of dreaming is pivotal when beginning a path of witchcraft, which seeks connection to the spiritual ecosystem. When we are asleep, our subconscious takes over, and we are freely connected to the spiritual ecosystem without the active mind stressing about daily tasks, or being influenced by conditioning that we have been subjected to throughout our lives. Instead we can simply listen to our soul, and information transmitted in dreams can be the vehicle for messages, memories from other incarnations, advice from ancestors, experiences with other spirits . . . the limitless potential within the dream state is fascinating.

Dreaming can almost be a type of spiritual counsel, for when we are conflicted in our lives, the answers may show up in dreams, or we may examine lurking shadow work there too. The symbolism may take some interpreting, and the answers are less straightforward than we might like, but wisdom can be found in this state.

Perhaps we are unknowingly connecting to our original soul for answers, wandering through an inner library of memories from this and many other incarnations, seeking answers within. Perhaps we are also so easily connected to all other spirits through the Cauldron of Wisdom that it begins to fill with cosmic knowledge we have convinced ourselves (for whatever reason) that we do not have.

We, as human spirits, are meant to be connected in an ecosystem, and the disconnect from our world is a source of great spiritual wounding. Much of the wisdom of our forebearers and spirits that are other than human has been lost to mainstream society. We live in a world that encourages a selfish mindset in terms of money and power—to harm anyone and anything as long as we succeed in terms that society has set for us. Our souls can therefore feel in conflict between the natural state of what it is to be a soul in the spiritual ecosystem—to care, to be connected, to be a guardian of nature—and the conditioning we receive to dominate, manipulate, and financially benefit ourselves at any cost. This conflict can manifest as dreams and nightmares, for in a sleeping state there is no denying what the soul feels.

Symptoms of being in conflict with a soul truth can manifest in despairingly not knowing who we are, feeling constantly disingenuous or at odds with our lives and other people in it. We do not feel authentic, and we are not even sure what "authentic" is meant to look or feel like. We might also feel a deep loathing for societal structures that are broken and hypocritical, designed to benefit a ruling wealthy elite at the cost of everyone and everything else in the world. The great soul divide in our reality—the choice of ecosystem and community versus selfishness.

All souls have some access to Awen, the force of inspiration that inspires us, at least up to the point where the psychopathic soul breaks from the spiritual ecosystem.

In the *Cauldron of Poesy* poem, it is stated that "Some say it is in the soul, for the body does nothing without the soul. Some say it is in the body were the arts are learned, passed through the bodies of our ancestors. It is said that this is the truth remaining over the root of poetry, and the wisdom in every person's ancestry does not come from the northern sky into everyone, but into every other person."[32]

The poem in addition questions whether the root of poetic inspiration is in the soul or the body—personally, I would suggest both. Awen is imprinted into the etheric body as the soul imprints at the point of birth and, in most cases, continues to flow through the soul via the spiritual ecosystem, influencing the auric body (through which to the mind and the physical self).

When no further supply of inspiration is available, an individual may become obsessive about behaving in a certain way over and over again, or perhaps there is seemingly no rhyme or reason to a person's choices. They are uninspired. The Cauldron of Wisdom can be polluted in this fashion, and knowledge is acquired for selfish gain with no consideration for anyone else. The process of transmuting knowledge into wisdom is lost.

It is, of course, possible to overcome the selfish conditioning of the world and have a spiritual awakening—not for full-blown psychopaths, but for people who have displayed some awful personality traits or made mistakes in the past and choose to change and put the work in to overcome this and become better people.

The more knowledge we have of this world and other people, the less likely we are to be hateful toward others. When a person is engaging with the energy of Awen through their soul, they will be inspired in different areas of their life at different times (although blockages can occur). The flow of Awen from the spiritual ecosystem is uninterrupted for the most part, and then that energetic flow also returns to the original soul. The deeper and more profound this connection, the more inspired a person will feel—and the closer to their purpose in this lifetime. They will feel inspired and fulfilled even when the soul work is challenging.

Blockages may occur due to social conditioning and pressures—as the mental stress from our lives can overwhelm us into feeling disconnected. This kind of disconnect is temporary, unlike the breaking from the spiritual ecosystem, and can be regained with rest, meditation, and alleviation of stress with counseling and healthy life choices.

Dreaming is the state where we can learn much about our souls, uninterrupted by the steady flow of conditioning from the world around us, and it is the way most people will experience a form of shapeshifting. In the realm of Sky, we can hear the whispering of our original soul, and the lessons it is learning or has learned so far. As we connect deeply to our own soul and seek to free ourselves from a solely selfish mindset, we begin to open ourselves up to the whispers across the hedge.

If you struggle to remember your dreams, try mugwort tea before bed! These blends are readily available from herbalists and spiritual stores, or you can create your own:

If you have foraged mugwort, make sure you wash it well before use. Boil a cup of water, and pour over chopped mugwort leaves. Leave to infuse for 10 minutes. Strain the fluid out into a mug and add sweetener if you prefer, such as locally sourced honey. Mugwort can be bitter, so honey or additional herbs added to it (such as mint) can make it more palatable.

Correspondences of the Cauldron of Wisdom

- Realm of Sky
- Connection to the flow of inspiration, Awen
- Key themes: Inspiration, mental well-being, spiritual power, dreams, breath
- Herbs:
    - Mugwort
    - Rosemary
    - Spruce
    - Pine
- Essential oils:
    - Rosemary
    - Lavender
    - Bergamot
    - Peppermint
- Trees:
    - Hazel
    - Apple
    - Oak

Hedge Witch Visualization: Cauldron of Wisdom and Sky

The following visualization is designed to help you connect to the Cauldron of Wisdom and the realm of Sky within yourself.

You will need:

- A cauldron (or substitute dark bowl)
- Some or all the herbs/tree materials, but if you have to choose between them, then mugwort, lavender, and rosemary are preferable and easily accessible
- One of the following incenses to stimulate the mind:
  - Peppermint
  - Frankincense
  - Spruce
  - Lavender
- Skin-safe anointing oil

For this exercise, we are going to be focusing on our breathing as a source of life force that connects us to all other spirits in our world and as a conduit of inspiration. With the assistance of the plants, herbs, and trees, we will seek to deepen our connection to the Cauldron of Wisdom located in the head.

In later chapters, we will seek to deepen our connection to the spirits of the natural world, so I recommend doing this activity before you attempt the later work, and afterward, to compare your results.

Have all the items in front of you on an altar space, table, or outside on the grass (with a blanket and a safe holder for the incense).

1. Before you begin take three deep, cleansing breaths, and pay attention to how this makes you feel. Breathe in deeply through your nose, filling your lungs, allowing your chest to expand, hold for a count of three, and then breathe out through your mouth.
2. Set your intention by stating out loud (or in your mind):

I have come to open the inner gate to wisdom.
I wish to connect to the Cauldron of Wisdom within and the realm of Sky.

3. Spend a moment observing the items in front of you. Observation is a spiritual practice of the Cauldron of Wisdom. It is the art and practice of perception without the need to impact. Societal conditioning teaches us that the need to be (aka feel) important is paramount—to weigh our worth measured by fame (by any means), by notoriety, by legacy, by impact. That being forgotten or forgettable is one of the worst fates imaginable, when in reality (or perhaps, beyond reality), nothing, and no one, no part of soul, is ever forgotten within the spiritual ecosystem. The act of observance in reverence to the cyclic nature of the earth and all her spirits attunes us to a more natural state. It allows us to "be" without performance.
4. Observe the herbs, plants, or tree material in front of you. Drink them in with your eyes. Note the depth of color and contours of the shape of each herb, any peculiarities, damage, or imperfections. Consider whether you have any memories with each plant—does it remind you of any time in your life?
5. Take each herb in your hand, and breathe in its scent. Scent is directly connected to memory, and this may stir something in your mind. Close your eyes and allow any memories or images to flow freely through you. Hold that image in your mind for a moment, and then open your eyes and place the herb into the cauldron (or bowl) in front of you. Repeat for each plant.
6. Once you have taken a deep breath of all the herbs, you can light your incense, which has been chosen to stimulate your mind.
7. Meditate in this space for a few moments, allowing yourself to relax and the stresses of the mundane world to fade away.
8. Once you feel calm, you may wish to ground, center, and release yourself. If you have a preferred method to do this, use that, but if not:

- To ground is to connect to the Land, to anchor your energy through the Earth.
- To center is to connect to the Sky, to open yourself to inspiration and spiritual truth.
- To release is to connect to the Sea, to energetically wash away that which blocks your vitality.

To Ground with the Realm of Sky

Visualize a gray/blue energetic swirling pool inside a cauldron that begins behind your mind's eye in your head. Breathe deeply and comfortably as you do so.

The pool may be swirling slowly, the color may be murky, and it may be vibrating with the stresses of everyday life. You may actually feel this pressure in your head.

Visualize a tendril of energy coming up from the swirling waters, as an energetic thread or a little river.

This thread extends over the lid of the cauldron, and comes down through your head, down through your body, seeking to return to the earth beneath you. It travels past a cauldron at the heart, and a cauldron at the stomach, and down into your legs.

Roots stretch out from your feet, down into the earth, and in this space we reflect the wisdom of the rooted plant spirits.

The gray thread travels through our roots, where it finds tendrils of energy coming up from the earth. We are connected to these earth-based roots, and the thread weaves itself around them, and an energy exchange takes place. We will discuss this in depth in the realm of Land, but for now, trust the process. Feel the excess of nervous, jittery energy flowing out from your mind into the earth, where it is alchemized, renewed, and rejuvenated.

Feel energy coming back up from the connection that fills your body with a sense of peace, connectedness, and mental harmony.

Visualize the energy returning up through your body to the Cauldron of Wisdom and filling it with this grounded energy.

The contents of the cauldron now swirl freely without blockage, and the color is clearer.

To Center with the Realm of Sky

Once more, visualize the Cauldron of Wisdom in your head.

To connect to the realm of Sky, chant or sing the word *Awen*, whichever you feel most comfortable with. Play with how the word sounds as you do so—try feeling inspired to extend certain syllables or pronunciations. Visualize the inner spiral of the cauldron shimmering with the power of Awen, glowing brighter as you do so.

To center is the natural state of the realm of Sky, and you are simply embodying the energy that is already present in the cauldron.

To Release with the Realm of Sky

As we breathe out, our breath and the water molecules within it return to the oniverse, and all rivers return to the source.

This is true on earth and in the spiritual ecosystem, where all rivers—tears, breath, words—return to the original self.

If you feel certain shadows are blocking you from connection to your soul self, your authenticity, then name them. Speak them out loud and as you do so, breathe out. I like to give an extra breath at the end of the exhale with a little "huh" noise and a clench in my stomach (the seat of the realm of Sea in the body), to ensure the release. Visualize the blockages being carried away through the air to the Sea, where they will dissolve in salt and water.

To conclude, look at the cauldron in front of you, full of herbs, trees, spirits, and energy. Observe it as a reflection of the cauldron in your mind, the Cauldron of Wisdom.

Take the skin-safe anointing oil, and draw a spiral on your forehead.

Speak the words: "I honor the Cauldron of Wisdom within me, that inspires me, and connects me to my highest spiritual self."

You may wish to incorporate these herbs into further hedge witchery especially for assisting in the realm of mental well-being, for memory recall, or dreaming. They would make an ideal ingredients when dried for a spell pouch to be placed under your pillow to encourage dream recall.

Anytime you need an affirmation to reconnect to this cauldron you may wish to use this:

I inspire.
I am inspired.
I am inspiring.
Words as soul rivers of breath.
Awen.
I inspire.

CAULDRON OF MOTION

"Moving and living the truth of our Soul, the Cauldron of Motion, initiated by grief and joy, guides us on our path in life. . . . it relates to living an engaged, truthful life . . . for many people, damaged by traumatic life events, this cauldron has become dormant and stagnant."[33]

The Cauldron of Motion is connected to the physical realm through which we embody and manifest all our experiences, our skills, where we alchemize the flow of creativity from the Awen into tangible results.

On the leg of the triskele, this is the realm of Land. In the shapeshifting realms, it is the middle realm, the one that is closest to our own, and according to the *Cauldron of Poesy*, is impacted and affected by our experiencing sorrow or joy, and seemingly more verses are dedicated to how this is accomplished than in any other section. This is likely due to nature, that the physical acts ascribed here are actions of life force, experiences to be had and remembered.

The Cauldron of Motion is said in the *Cauldron of Poesy* to be moved (and moveable) through the feelings of sorrow and joy, and I personally feel that this is the expression of emotions relating to life force and death force, forces which are always impacting the soul.

When it comes to lessons of death, the Celtic goddess Morrigan in her aspect of Badb has been pivotal to my understanding of them, and she is also intrinsically connected to the realm of Land (more on this later). If one lesson has struck me to the core when it comes to spirit work with the Morrigan, it is of Badb and memory, for in meditative journey work she told me, "We are all the moments of death we carry with us."

The connection between the realm of Land in its deep, dark cavernous form, its manifestation which is expressed in dance, the experiencing of life and death force in our soul, all culminates in the diverse emotional responses we have to living out our lives and experiencing beginnings and endings.

Within our lives we experience the greatest moments of the emotion of sorrow that is formed in grieving. Whether this is grieving the loss of a person, animal, or idea, the result is the same, a deep wave of lasting sorrow imprinted onto our memory and, perhaps, our soul.

This in turn creates an energetic link between mourner and the person (or animal, idea) who has moved on. A piece of death is then carried within the mourner in their grief, and a piece of life is carried within the person who died so that they could be reborn—a balancing exchange in the scope of energy and memory that impacts souls that have weaved a part of the fabric of their being into one another.

If this is so, then this is one way in which we carry the energetic imprint of our ancestors within us, and these links create pathways to connect with other spirits in the spiritual ecosystem, or middle realm. Whether consciously or not, we all carry these small fingerprints within our energetic matrix, tethering us to those who lived and died so that we might live.

I consider the acts of living and dying to not be separate but to coexist within ourselves at all points of our journey. We are constantly engaging in death cycles and being reborn; at the same time, the outer shell is always dying and regenerating over a lifespan that gradually degrades, until we are spent—though incarnation death can come at any time. Only the Morrigan has the foresight to know that, guarding my death as she does, and that is just as well. Such knowledge would likely drive us mad.

Instead, it is the knowing of the death force which reminds us of the life force within—the premise of "memento mori" (remember that you shall die), a lesson that comes with the balance of "memento vivere"—remember to live. Remember that you too will die, so live.

In recent years the collective consciousness has been littered with consequences of so many deaths, both in the physical realm and of what has gone before as old institutions and traditions crumble. It has been an energy of bare bones and stark realizations, showing where the rot has crept in and must be washed down before the body can be buried. Many have rejoined the earth, and still more hear the land and its people mourning. Feeling our ancestors encroaching on our memory, for all that we have forgotten—desperate to impart something like wisdom, or knowledge at least.

Remember that you are dying, and what is left behind is our legacy, how we will be remembered.

How many of us have become acutely aware of how much of our lives were devoted to the service of busyness, starving ourselves to fill the bellies of someone else, constantly putting our needs at the bottom of a heap? I have become aware of the act of living, the choices of living, the awareness of living—and in so doing honoring the lifeblood in my veins, which speaks to a line a thousand strong of people who died so that I might live. Their voices call out across the spiritual ecosystem to embody and manifest the idea of memento vivere within our lives—to seek joyous experience and memories.

I become aware of the squandering of precious moments engaged in negative cycles, worrying over meaningless trivial notions, tied up in caring for those who did not care about me, and how I had bled my pages dry when I had so much more that I could say. I submerge myself into the blood pool of my own creative spirit womb (which I consider completely separate to any physical womb—everyone can have one, it is simply the Cauldron of Motion).

The essence of life force, of joy turning the Cauldron of Motion, is the beating heart of what it means to truly be alive, the great gift of opportunity and time, and getting aligned with what makes us feel emboldened and emblazoned.

What stokes the fire of your personal passion?

Burn away that which truly does not matter. Let the toxic threads that strangle be done.

The Expression of the Cauldron of Motion

If the Cauldron of Motion is tied to the living and dying experience of us all, then it is also the cauldron tied to the manifestation of those experiences—how we live out the memories we are making.

We can connect to the Otherworlds through the Cauldron of Motion through the land, and one way in which to do this is within earthbound spaces such as caves or burial sites such as Celtic barrows. Technically, these are grave sites that connect the world of the living to that of the dead—which is exactly the dynamic just described as playing out within ourselves in our psyche and memory.

I find the idea of the grave an intriguing one, with its dual meaning now referencing a physical location for the deceased as well as an emotional expression, which is arguably the death of all joy. The etymology of *grave* is straightforward with one or two interesting tidbits:

> "Excavation in earth for reception of a dead body," Old English *græf* "grave; ditch, trench; cave," from Proto-Germanic *grafa-/graba-* (source also of Old Saxon *graf*, Old Frisian *gref*, Old High German

grab "grave, tomb," Old Norse *gröf* "cave," Gothic *graba* "ditch"), cognate with Old Church Slavonic *grobu* "grave, tomb," and perhaps from a [Proto-Indo-European] root **ghrebh-* "to dig, to scratch, to scrape," related to Old English *grafan* "to dig."[34]

I find the nuance of "cave" here of particular interest, because it crosses the divide of places that are associated with being entrances to the Otherworld, such as Oweynagat (Uaimh na gCat), which is one of the sacred sites of the Morrigan and from which she is said to emerge each Samhain.

In this sense, the intermingling between graves and caves are certainly places firmly within the human psyche as not necessarily simply places of death but of transition. A grave is a physical location of a deceased shell of a person but is also a symbol of another doorway, one we have dug ourselves into the realm of Land so that body may decompose and rejoin the earth as the spirit crosses over and rejoins the Otherworld.

Caves then are the natural formation version of a grave, which allow passage to and from the realm of spirits and the gods, and as such, the Morrigan, in her role as Death Goddess, rises from this gateway on Samhain, the sacred Celtic day associated with the dead. The two also mirror one another with the idea of immortality and eternity. There is usually a link to the Otherworld attributed to this—that time moves differently in the realm of the dead or Otherworld—

> The belief in rebirth was strong in the Celtic world . . . naturally tied in with the notion of another world. The belief also provided a comforting impression of continuity. The dead were not altogether gone. . . . From the Otherworld, those who had gone before watched and protected their descendants and took an interest in the communities that they had left.[35]

Graves are usually places of mourning, marked with a tombstone or equivalent dressings, in order that a person may be remembered. The idea is that it marks the world with a footprint that lends an ounce of immortality to a person. This was even more typified in the ancient Celtic barrows—monuments of stone dedicated to the deceased which appear as though artificial caverns under mounds of earth. In both cases, however, there is a sobering thought: Are either of these circumstances eternal in truth? Are they eternal if there is no one left who remembers them?

For my part, I feel that they are an eternal part of the spiritual ecosystem regardless of whether those who are incarnate in this realm remember—and even should the realm collapse in on itself at the end of its cycle, the spiritual ecosystem is the nexus between all planes of existence.

Memory is imprinted into the spiritual ecosystem, and it remembers. Memory is the true grave—a place that opens the gateway between the realms of the living and the dead, something we can tap into as witches. In the realm of Land, our bodies are the embodiment of memory, the physical markers left on us by our ancestors through DNA.

It is also worth considering how the land and the cave spaces within that land are considered the domain of the divine feminine and are often aligned to mother energy and the concept of womb-space-birthing. Our planet is referred to as Mother Earth, even by people who have no inclination toward spiritual practice, as is the idea that without her we could not live, which of course has roots in the mundane reality. If the earth becomes damaged beyond repair the human race will die out permanently in the manifested realm.

Caverns are linked to genitalia because of the resemblance they bear, but I prefer the analysis that they are simply both gateways of life force. I work with the idea of energetic womb spaces to allow the energy work of the hedge witch to be inclusive, so whether or not you have a physical womb you can honor and connect to this energy within the self. You can even ditch the term if you prefer and replace it with "cavern of soul" or stick with the cauldron analogy.

Physically birthing children is not an option for everyone, nor is it some people's choice, but that does not mean that they cannot connect to the birthing process in the spirit realm. Whether you birth children, ideas, poetry, inspiration, or manifestations of your soul's work, all should feel deeply connected in the realm of Land.

You are worthy, and you are welcome here.

The emotions of joy and sorrow are what turn the Cauldron of Motion. Joy and sorrow as expressions of self can be found within life and within death, and all our emotional responses are valid. To state there is only sorrow in grief is an oversimplification of the emotional cycle attached to that experience. Relief and joy in the memories of a loved one are two quick examples of how joy can find its way into the experiencing of death force.

As we honor our emotions, our time, and our memories, we honor the act of living and dying—that which connects all spirits across the hedge.

Correspondences of the Cauldron of Motion

- Realm of Land
- Connection to the flow of life and death forces
- Key themes: Embodiment, emotions, physical self-manifesting our experience
- Herbs:
  - Rose
  - Motherwort
  - Garlic
- Essential oils:
  - Oregano
  - Rose
  - Patchouli
  - Vetiver
- Trees:
  - Hawthorn
  - Yew
  - Silver birch

Deepening Our Understanding of the Cauldron of Motion: Grounding and Healing with the Land and the Sacred

What is the magical practice of grounding or "earthing"? Most will describe a process of channeling an excess of energy away from the auric body into the ground, so you feel more anchored to reality, less jittery, more yourself. Grounding does this, but in my mind, that is not what earthing actually is—that is the result of it.

Earthing is a two-way connection to the spirit of the land through our energetic roots that brings us into closer alignment with the ultimate sacred grove, the spiritual ecosystem. The land is our planet's manifestation of the spiritual ecosystem—spirit life force given many shapes, forms, textures, scents, languages. Given the limitless nature of the spiritual ecosystem, I believe there to be limitless expressions of it: different planets and worlds with ecosystems that look different from ours, speak different languages, and so forth. But as we incarnated on this planet, that is meant to be our sensory experience in this incarnation!

When we ground, we acknowledge that we are our own sacred space, a mini sacred grove, reaching out for nourishment from the larger sacred space. An energy exchange occurs, and we return to a balanced state, where our soul rivers are giving and receiving at the same time. The memories of the spirits of the land can flow freely into us, harmonizing us with their song. We may not be fully aware of what they are saying, and sometimes it's best not to overload ourselves with too much information, but we do benefit from the feeling of that connectedness. We harmonize with the larger ecosystem. We enter the soul stillness. We become the land. Grounding and connection to the earth are considered vital for physical and spiritual healing.

Embodiment is another spiritual practice of the Cauldron of Motion which is part of the grounding process. It is a necessity to connect back to our land, the spirits there, and find a kind of peace is paramount in the modern world. We remember this when we seek out the beauty of nature, when we go for walks or adventures or vacations. We are engaging in soul-muscle-memory with these actions. We seek out the sacred and safe spaces in nature, because they speak to our souls. When we reconnect our soul and body with the spirits of the land, we embody this connection—take it into ourselves and manifest it.

At home we might reconnect to this sensation by regularly grounding.

Hedge Witch Visualization: Cauldron of Motion and Land

There are many topics of personal healing that we can consider: forest bathing, walking off the stress, natural herbalism in all its forms, and so on. By engaging with our bodies and the body of the land, we help deepen that connection and balance our Cauldron of Motion.

The following visualization is designed to help you connect to the Cauldron of Motion and the realm of Land within yourself.

You will need:

- A cauldron (or substitute dark bowl)
- Some or all the herbs/tree materials, but if you have to choose between them, then rose and hawthorn are preferable and easily accessible
- One of the following incenses to anchor the body
- Rose
  - Oregano
  - Sage
  - Patchouli
- Skin-safe anointing oil

For this exercise, we are going to be focusing on our body and its sensations as a vessel of life force and death force that connects us to all other spirits in our world and as a conduit of emotional manifestation. With the assistance of the plants, herbs, and trees, we will seek to deepen our connection to the Cauldron of Motion located in the chest.

In later chapters we will seek to deepen our connection to the spirits of the natural world, so I recommend doing this activity before you attempt the later work, and afterward, to compare your results.

Have all the items in front of you on an altar space, table, or outside on the grass (with a blanket and a safe holder for the incense).

1. Before you begin, take three deep, cleansing breaths, and pay attention to how this makes you feel. Breathe in deeply through your nose, filling your lungs, allowing your chest to expand, hold for a count of three, and then breathe out through your mouth.
2. Set your intention by stating out loud (or in your mind):
   I have come to open the inner gate of embodiment. I wish to connect to the Cauldron of Motion within and the realm of Land.
3. For this cauldron, we are focusing on the tactile feel of each of the herbs. Hold them between your hands, and note the sensations of each herb, its texture, how its spirit chooses to manifest in our reality. Place each herb into the cauldron in front of you and then place your

hands over your heart, asking for the healing power of the herbs to transfer within your body.

This meditative journey was channeled via the spiritual ecosystem and the goddess Morrigan. It is about creating equilibrium to give your auric body "solid ground" on which to begin protection spellwork.

The mental image is superimposed over the physical body as the Morrigan showed me in meditation. There are two intersecting triskeles of energy with the space between them forming a diamond shape. This space is the gateway through which nourishing energy from the spiritual ecosystem enters the person at the heart space (where the Cauldron of Motion is located). This acts as a doorway—a cave entrance—through which healing, cleansing, nourishing energy comes flooding in to balance the auric and physical self.

> Visualize a tree above you, and another beneath you. The tree above you is upright, roots descending toward you, and the tree beneath you is inverted, its roots reaching upward toward you. These two trees are connection points to the spiritual ecosystem.
>
> You visualize healing mint-green light descending through the roots of the tree above, coming down through the triskele, into yourself.
>
> Your body glows and identifies any blockages, wounds, or stagnant energies. These appear as dark spots, knots, tears, and so forth—the manifestation of the spiritual blockages within the body. Breathe in deeply as you take energy into your body.
>
> The energy unknots, cleanses, stitches back together, heals as the nourishing energy from the spiritual ecosystem unites in your auric body.
>
> The tree beneath your body is the vessel to clear away energy to be renewed in the spiritual ecosystem. The roots carry away any energetic nastiness, anything that needs banishing or cleansing out. Between the two points the body forms a circuit, so energy is balanced within you (there is no deficit).
>
> You visualize murky icky energy (like sludge) being carried out of your body into the roots below. There, alchemy occurs. The roots absorb and break down the sludge energy, breaking it apart until it is

transformed into fluid energy again, and carries on down through the roots into the ecosystem. Breathe out deeply as this energy leaves your body.

Both triskeles glowed gold/white/green when I saw them, which I believe is part of the cleansing and healing process. They would manifest differently if they were being used to create different energy matrices for other purposes—for example, black would be for spiritual energy work of absorption/banishing/protection.

As the triskele is a symbol of all three realms, Land, Sea, and Sky spirits are already present in this meditation. As a reminder:

- To ground is to connect to the land to anchor your energy through the earth.
- To center is to connect to the sky, to open yourself to inspiration and spiritual truth.
- To release is to connect to the sea, to energetically wash away that which blocks your vitality.

Within the triskele meditation the main focus is the spirits of Land, to ground your energy into the earth by using the spiritual ecosystem as a conduit for balance and healing. As you are centered within the ecosystem, your breath connects you to the realm of Sky. The energy that is unblocked and carried away from you also provides the release from the realm of Sea. You may find that you need a cry when certain blockages are released. This is normal, release as you need to!

Following the healing visualization, ground your body further with nourishment of a healthy snack. Apple slices are ideal, for example.

To conclude: Look at the cauldron in front of you, full of herbs, trees, spirits, and energy. Place your hands around it and know that it represents a reflection of the cauldron in your heart space, the Cauldron of Motion. Take the skin-safe anointing oil, and draw a spiral on your chest. Speak the words: "I honor the Cauldron of Motion within me, through which my emotions manifest and connect me to my heart."

You may wish to incorporate these herbs into further hedge witchery—especially for assisting in the realm of emotion well-being, honoring loved ones or ancestors, or in spells of joy or sorrow. They would make ideal ingredients when dried for a spell of emotional release.

Any time you need an affirmation to reconnect to this cauldron, you may wish to use this:

I feel.
I am emotion.
I am emotional.
Sensation as soul rivers of touch.
Awen.
I emote.

THE CAULDRON OF WARMING

My perfect cauldron of warming,
has been taken by the Gods from the mysterious abyss of the elements;
a perfect truth that ennobles from the center of being,
That pours forth a terrifying stream of speech.
. . . for Eber Donn, the making of fearful poetry,
Of vast mighty draughts death-spells.[36]

The Cauldron of Warming is connected to our vitality, the wellspring of life force that is the point of the wild animalistic self, tied to the rivers of our blood that transport vitality around the body. As a result, it is also tied to death, that which occurs when all our life fluid runs out.

On the leg of the triskele, this is the realm of Sea. Within the self, there are many rivers, and the circulatory system is one of these. Within the realm of Sea, there are many themes: how all rivers flow back to the ocean, the eternal depths of the unknowable self—much like the unknowable depths of the sea and the wellspring of knowledge that flows through our Cauldron of Warming.

Eber Donn, in the poem above, is associated by some with the Celtic god of the dead due to the fact they are both associated with Tech Duinn (the Celtic Underworld), and is said to have been the chief of the Milesian invaders who set out to conquer ancient Ireland. Eber Donn died in a shipwreck—in the sea—because of magic conjured by the Danaan people.[37]

John Shaw, writing about the folklore of Ireland and Scotland, notes that the ultimate death, being the apocalypse, is given in these Celtic texts as the realms of Land, Sea, and Sky being out of balance:

> One character, or two (in some variants a hen, in others human) receives a signal that the sky is about to fall on the earth, or simply the approach of death (bás) or doom (bráth). In some variants they are down by the shore, and are made aware of the impending disaster by being struck by an object falling from the sky. They set out to carry the news to others (animals or human) in succession, all of whom bear distinctive, often comical names, using a formula along the lines of: "Who has seen or heard it?" "My eyes have seen it, my ears have heard it, my soles have felt it." They form a growing procession as they go through the country until they reach a destination of sorts: in many variants a white horse carries them to a river where they are drowned.[38]

We should note that the final moment of death is by water—the river. Rivers were thought of as being important liminal spaces in Celtic mythology, where one could gain access to the Otherworld.

The mythology and legends of rivers throughout Europe are immense. The folklore of each river is often tied into its name, with the creation of many of them being due to the bodily fluid of a god or goddess or other mythic creature, be that by urination, blood, tears, or sweat.

With the spiritual ecosystem and on earth there are many rivers that flow from the point of creation, of which the Irish goddess Danu would be one. Danu is said to be the Mother Goddess of the Tuatha Dé Danann, meaning "people of Danu." Her name may derive from the Proto-Indo-European root *$d^h enh_2$ (to run, to flow) and is associated with the river Danube. The Welsh figure Dôn (mother of Gwydion and Arianrhod, and sister of Math ap Mathonwy) seems to be a cognate, who gives her name to the rivers Don in Yorkshire and Aberdeen, but precious little else remains from the ancient texts on either of these goddesses.

Both goddesses are associated with being the mother of gods, and thus would be the point of creation, the primordial creatrix, who is the hub, nexus, or spring of a spiritual pantheon. From her, all rivers flow. The rivers are of water but also of life force (blood and energy) and spiritual tendrils and energetic maps.

I feel that we, as humans, are a blueprint for this also—as we connect back to the goddess Danu we become physical landmarks in the same way a physical location on earth can be. We have mountain regions, we are creatures made of water, earth, and a little stardust. Our minds are mirrors to the universe, the brain and mind space being universe creation given flesh. We move through energy fields (rivers of energy) all day without even noticing, and at night we swim among the stars of our subconscious.

The energies of the realm of Sea are often tied to the moon, which so affects the tides, and how we, being made up largely of water, are impacted as a result. This correlates to the lower realm within shapeshifting. Water can represent the deep places within, as rivers of time are another way of looking at the root system of the spiritual ecosystem.

The lessons within the realm of Sea are all about the water that flows around us and within us—how we remember, reconnect, and release, of memory, of ancestral lines, of nourishment, of all the journeys led by water and rain.

The emotional state cannot be hidden behind a dam, for in the restriction it only festers, and from the Cauldron of Warming the unconscious connects, bringing with it echoes of other lives.

Water too is dangerous, and it carries all the memories of every spirit ever wronged within its depths, not because of death (which is natural) but rather the abhorrent disregard for the life within. How many times have we disregarded our well-being for convenience? For the benefit of others who never thank us, who drain us beyond our limits? How many times are we forced into a comfortable-shaped vial by the dictation of society so that we might fit and be drunk down in manageable gulps?

Are we meant to be swallowed whole? Shouldn't they drown in the richness of our being, those that are determined to drink of us?

I feel the power of every kind of river that is behind the veil and within our world calling out across the spiritual ecosystem. Rivers of memory that span across culture and time, knowing no divides, flowing in and out of the universe, splashing at the memory banks to keep us soaked in the kisses of our ancestors.

Remember: the ancestors call to us, reminding us of their lives and how they lived and poured our essence into us like a river.

The moon reminds us of the repressed and the repressive, that which lurks beneath the surface and we have tried (and will fail) to ignore. There is no more swimming in shallows, starlet, plunge into your richness, your depth. Use this affirmation:

Cry.
Let the rivers flow from my eyes.
Scream.
Let the rivers flow from my lungs.
Weave.
Let the rivers flow from my fingertips.
Love.
Let the rivers flow from my heart.

The ocean itself is primal, the primordial soup from which all life started, and the Celts believed in which all life will end. There is a heaviness in the ocean. As the waves rumble overhead, it can feel as though the pressure of the entire ocean is pressing down on our shoulders when we connect with it. Heavy and isolating. It's like Alice being swirled around in an ocean of her own making, one that she cried into existence.

Tears are cleansing, they carry out the misery from our bodies and the painful sting from our memories, until all that remains is the numb feeling of floating underwater, wondering how we ended up here. It becomes a cocoon, the sadness we have cried. It wraps us in the amniotic fluid of the primordial Mother Goddess swirling us in her abyss-deep depths. We cannot cry or scream anymore, to do so would just gulp down the salt tear water we have already surrounded ourselves with. The poison is purged, and here we float as our wounds sting and begin to close.

Someday soon we will be reborn and emerge, breaking the horizon line into a thousand pieces, breathing desperately of our fullest potential. Knowing that we can survive this too, as we always have before. A thousand tears that marked our faces when we couldn't hold on any longer, and all that we could do was release.

The act of surrender. The struggle to let go. How human of us it is to struggle against the tide, to think for a moment we can exert our control here, and the gods of the ocean simply smile and wash us out to sea with a wink. Sailors' shanties ring heavy in the air, tales of travel across the unfathomable depths, as monsters eye us from underneath—and perhaps they do, all those inner demons we have maligned and shunned, the parts of self we label and hide away, the parts that tear, and rip, and growl, and shriek.

If we are to love the broken things, we should probably start with the broken parts of ourselves, the ocean whispers, and we are left puzzled as to when the notion of broken became negative and undesirable. A thousand scattered seeds will travel the air currents and increase their chance to germinate and grow.

So too can our thoughts, hurting, be cast out to the wind and carry us across oceans of time into our limitless natures. You are raw potential manifested, surrounded by the tears that will salt the earth of the past so you might never go back there, and tear through into a new existence.

Elemental Spirits

To attune with the elemental spirits I believe it is necessary to reconsider our relationship to them. Many of us in the beginning of our path may have spent time connecting to the elements as prescribed in many, many Witchcraft 101 books. I want us to connect to the primal essence of each realm, much in the same way I describe the "All" spirit when connecting to a plant or tree, I want to find the eternal essence for each element and bring that into our embodiment.

They already exist within us, of course, because there is no real separation in the spiritual ecosystem except where we create (or perceive) it to be. To connect is therefore the act of remembering that we are both separate and connected all at once. We can be self-contained individuals as well as being part of the interconnected ecosystems (physical and spiritual).

It is putting aside the manmade doubts that the elements are alive, conscious, and have connected spirit. This is an exercise in and of itself, to unpack the conditioning our world has instilled in us since we were children.

I believe it begins with a simple act: daring to consider this is a possibility. Allowing yourself to be open-minded. Disregarding whether or not people are silently judging you or what others might think. Considering that we are not alone in the universe, and we are not at the top of the food chain. Then sitting in meditation, or walking in meditation, and allowing your conscious mind to drift a little. Allow your psychic senses to click open and reach out into the expansiveness of the spiritual ecosystem—the unseen realms—calling out to something primal and largely forgotten by humankind.

To embody is to draw these elements into the self. Let us consider the primal essence of water—the realm of Sea, the element connected to the Cauldron of Warming at the base of our being.

In Irish, the word *coire* means both "cauldron" and "whirlpool." Thus the cauldrons are both the container and the substance, both contained and uncontained.

We will begin the meditation at our Cauldron of Warming, and move toward being submerged and surrounded by the ocean as we energetically journey through the cauldron.

Cauldron of Warming and Sea Exercise

Close your eyes and breathe deeply. Relax. Let the mundane world fade away. Use meditative music if that helps. Shift your energy inward, seek the tendril of soul that connects you to the spiritual ecosystem.

Begin by allowing your consciousness to drop into heart space—within yourself. Move down from this space to where your Cauldron of Warming is seated in your stomach, at the base of your auric being.

Connect with the spiritual ecosystem at your base, in what some call the root chakra or the (spirit) womb cauldron. You can also spread your roots through your feet energy centers. Pull these threads of energy upward into the Cauldron of Warming.

Visualize this cauldron within you, swirling a spiral inward into its center. The liquid within may be dark red, and you can make out slight waves within it.

Seek the spirit of water, the realm of Sea. Visualize the ocean in your mind, focus your intention on finding the spirit. Step inwardly into the center of the cauldron.

Find yourself within the ocean, able to comfortably breathe. Should you feel panicked at any time, know that you can come back into yourself. You are tethered to your body. Reach out for the essence of the primal spirit of water.

It is likely that you will not visualize a body for the primal essence, because the connective thread of all water spirit is so vast and all-encompassing. We are seeking connection, rather than conversation, for this element.

> Feel the essence of the element around your body: the lapping of waves, the coolness, perhaps the pressure against your body. Depending on how deep you are in the ocean, you may see light refracting through from the surface, and the unfathomable depths beneath you.
>
> You may seek ocean wildlife, but they pay you no mind, for you're traveling in the etheric realm and are of little interest to them.
>
> You might wish to swim, or simply float, and experience this energy for yourself.
>
> It is ageless. All knowing, and yet we know so little of it. A mystery. Vital. Necessary. Sometimes benevolent, sometimes ferocious.
>
> The energy that began life, and the energy that will end it.
>
> Feel the water that flows through your own body beating in response, your blood, your tears, your sweat. All the rivers that flow through you, connected at the base to the element of water, to the realm of Sea.
>
> Pull a small thread of the energy that surrounds you toward you, creating a ripple through the ocean that connects at your Cauldron of Warming.
>
> Connect.
>
> Be cleansed by it.
>
> Release.
>
> For nothing is so troublesome that the ocean cannot wash it away.
>
> Salt clears away everything, by sweat, tears, or the ocean.
>
> And so it is.

Your experiences may vary—all are valid! You may need several attempts to connect with and embody this energy. But you will feel more grounded into reality and deepen your psychic senses each time you attempt this.

Correspondences of the Cauldron of Warming

- Realm of Sea
- Connection to the blood, memory in the water, releasing

- Key themes: Release and surrender, memory from past lives
- Herbs:
  - Marshmallow root
  - Burdock
  - Dandelion
  - Cinnamon
- Essential oils:
  - Spikenard
  - Lemon balm
  - Marjoram
  - Vetiver
- Trees:
  - Willow
  - Ash
  - Alder

Hedge Witch Visualization: Cauldron of Warming and Sea

The following visualization is designed to help you connect to the Cauldron of Warming and the realm of Sea within yourself.

You will need:

- A glass tumbler or cup filled with drinking water
- An unscented blue or sea green candle
- One of the following incenses to assist with release:
  - Juniper
  - Mugwort
  - Spruce
- Skin-safe anointing oil

For this exercise, we are going to be focusing on release, particularly of blockages that are caused by inherited trauma or from past (alternate) lives. With the assistance of the plants, herbs, and trees we will seek to deepen our connection to the Cauldron of Warming, located in the stomach.

In later chapters, we will seek to deepen our connection to the spirits of the natural world, so I recommend doing this activity before you attempt the later work, and afterward, to compare your results.

Have all the items in front of you on an altar space, table, or outside on the grass (with a blanket and a safe holder for the incense).

1. Draw the triskele on a piece of paper and call forth the energies of the realm of Sea.
2. Tape this sigil onto a glass or place it underneath, and fill the glass with spring water. Affirm: "As the water begins its journey from the spring, so too do I."
3. Visualize the water churning with all of the power of the ocean.
4. Speak out loud the release that you are seeking, how you wish this cycle of your life to change you. You may say something like: "I wish to be released from this soul tether, known or unknown." Allow these words to flow from the heart, revealing every emotion. If you need to cry or scream, then do so. Your emotions and thoughts are the rivers of soul that will carry you forward, and you can't hide them from the universe anyway!
5. Light an unscented blue or sea green candle near the glass, as well as your incense, and call forth the releasing power of the sea. I often chant the Ogham Mor, which is a modern addition to the Celtic system but represents the ocean nonetheless. Mor has etymological roots associated with the ocean anyway, particularly from Wales. You can also use Muir, from the Irish tradition.
6. Let the water sit for an hour. You may wish to cover it. Once that time has passed, raise the glass and thank the realm of Sea.
7. Drink the water. Stand still and feel the impact of the energy flowing through your body. Sometime later you will release that water from your body, back to water—another river.

Any time you need an affirmation to reconnect to this cauldron you may wish to use this:

I bleed.
I am memory.
I am remembrance.
Memory as soul rivers of ecosystem.
Awen.
I recall.

By connecting to the three cauldrons within your energy field, you strengthen your psychic abilities, and balance your auric body. By doing so, will become more grounded, centered, and aligned with the spiritual ecosystem.

This will help you with astral journey work through the ecosystem, to connect with and speak to other spirits. By being more balanced, you will feel more confident in your intuition and recognizing spirit messages.

THE SACRED GROVE

Seneca, a philosopher of Stoicism in ancient Rome, surmised in his *Moral Epistles* a connection to the sacred grove: "When you enter a grove peopled with ancient trees, higher than the ordinary, and shutting out the sky with their thickly intertwined branches, do not the stately shadows of the wood, the stillness of the place, and the awful gloom of this doomed cavern then strike you with the presence of a deity?"[39]

The sacred grove is the inner sanctum, the sacred circle, the place where you can hear the whispers of the gods through the rustle of the leaves on the trees. It is a place of wonder, awe, and magic, where any individual can feel at peace with their place in the great cycles. Trees are ancient and wise, watchers of times gone by and all that has left to be. They speak of home not just in the physical sense but of the intricate interwoven energies that create a harmonious ecosystem, and that ecosystem outside of oneself reflects that within oneself—as within, so without.

Home for me is not a physical place. In the odd life I have had, physical places never seem to last. Instead, learning to be at home in one's own skin is of paramount importance. If you can be home for yourself, you will never be truly lost.

On the Celtic witchcraft path, Caim is the creation of an energetic circle of protection around one's self to keep you safe from all negativity and harm. Caim embodies and radiates the energy which I perceive as being the Celtic "temple"—that is, the sacred grove, a sacred space surrounded by and protected with tree and earth energy, a natural energy of peace and worship. This is, however, more of an astral journey and the creation of astral security—an ethereal thought-grove to help one access messages from the higher self and the Divine.

The ancient Druids of the Celtic people were known to have performed their rites in forests, particularly in sacred groves. In his work *Blood and Mistletoe,* Ronald Hutton describes the (albeit problematic) relaying of this information by the Romans, particularly the Roman poet Lucan:

> He portrayed the Druidae in Caesar's time as leaders of a tradition of "barbarous rites" . . . their rites were declared to have been carried on in the depths of forests. . . . [Caesar] ordered the grove to be felled. His men hesitated to touch the sacred trees. . . . Lucan could not resist embellishing it with a lurid description of the grove itself: "interlacing boughs enclosed a space of darkness and cold shadows . . . gods were worshipped there with savage rites. . . every tree was sprinkled with human blood. . . the branches moved of their own accord . . . yew trees fell and rose again, phantom flames appeared among the trunks."[40]

This account is a perfect example of the problematic nature of historical sources, especially when you consider that groves were sacred to the ancient Greeks and Romans. The agenda and bias are clear, but it does suggest at least a firm belief in the sacred groves of the ancient Druids.

Modern druids are quite happy to reclaim the idea, taking it back to its likely more historically accurate beginnings: "Druids today continue this tradition of seeking tranquil clearings in woods and forests, in which to meditate and hold ceremonies. And in addition, many contemporary Druids are creating new sacred groves—in their gardens, on their farms, or on public land."[41]

Forest and woodland spaces, and the sacred groves within them, inspire the soul. We can feel something other when we enter them . . . even if we cannot fully explain that sensation. They are liminal—a place full of nature and her spirits. It is speaking to a place deep within our own souls.

In ancient times, the Celtic people gathered here to pass laws, to create new ones, to hold religious ceremonies or those pertaining to sovereignty and the ruler of their people. The gravitas of these spaces is remembered in the earth, and through the spiritual ecosystem throughout time. Groves, forests, hedges . . . all align into the same energy—liminal spaces of nature that capture something of the spiritual heartbeat of the universe. Something we can all feel, because it already exists within us.

THE INNER SACRED GROVE

This concept is one I have arrived at as part of my pathwalking with Celtic hedge witchery.

The inner sacred grove is the internal embodiment of a sacred grove. It is a mix of visualization, acknowledging the inner ecosystem of the body as a reflection of the universe, and a method of reclaiming the sacred within the self. Conditioning over generations of religious doctrine has insisted that the body is separate from the Divine. Given the Pagan tendency to revere nature as an intrinsic part of divinity, it becomes necessary to reject any conditioning that insists we are separate from nature.

Although humans have done their best to destroy nature and set up isolation housing away from its inconveniences, we cannot escape that the natural state of things is to live as part of an ecosystem, and as we destroy them, ultimately, we destroy ourselves.

Visualizing Your Inner Sacred Grove

Try this activity in your journal to help you visualize your inner sacred grove.

Using a stick person model, draw elements that you would like present in your inner sacred grove as part of your body. What trees would be a part of your ecosystem? What would your roots look like? For example, I wanted fly agaric mushrooms on my shoulders, ivy across my body, and plenty of moss!

When you start to think about why you make those choices, it is a good indicator of who you are on a soul level and which plant/tree spirits you might be drawn to and why. This provides you with a gateway—a liminal space—for connecting to the spirits throughout the spiritual ecosystem that can best assist you when it comes to your spiritual needs. This can be an indicator of what kind of healing, grounding, or connection work might be in the best interests of your auric body.

There is a crossover here between the elements your inner ecosystem (your inner sacred grove) requires and the medicine that can be found within nature (the outer sacred grove or forest spaces). Plant spirit medicine is meant to be used in balance with modern medicine (which is often birthed from nature anyway).

When we go within ourselves, what do we see? Remember you are the container for the most intense form of sacred energy.

Inner Journey

Set up your usual meditative state ready to journey inward, making sure you are comfortable and will not be disturbed. You can add forest sounds or music if you are sitting inside.

You can also go into the forest and do active meditation. By walking through woodland spaces you are performing a natural exchange of energy—the ideal grounding or earthing. You are releasing any stress through exertion (even light walking) and that kinetic energy is released, and then you are absorbing the energy all around you from nature.

We are traveling inward. Focus on the Cauldron of Motion at your heart space, pulling your energy into that cauldron. Visualize your consciousness descending down into it. This is the Cauldron of Land, and from it we travel to our inner landscape.

> You see a cast-iron cauldron with nature growing out of it from within. It is full of herbs, and ferns, and trees, and roots . . . hinting at what is in your inner sacred grove. You may wish to try and remember which plants/trees stand out here to you to research later.
>
> Now you step inside the cauldron. You climb down into it, traveling deep down into it, down through your body, using the plant life as a guide, until you find the base of the cauldron. You push up and float up through the cauldron on the other side—the cauldron within yourself. The two are connected like a tunnel.
>
> As you come up out of it, you will find yourself in your inner sacred grove.

Later we will use this visualization of your inner grove to draw a sacred grove as part of our circle casting for spellcraft in hedge witchcraft. This is the process of materializing your inner sacred grove outside of the body as sacred space. Your inner witchcraft, your magic, your power, will flow out through your cauldrons, your arms, your being . . . and you energetically create a sacred grove around you as sacred liminal space, stepping between worlds as you do so, which is also stepping into yourself.

As you enter into the sacred grove of yourself, what do you see, feel, and hear?

Be honest . . . do some things need tending to? Are parts in need of attention, pruning, trimming back? Are any leaves diseased? Are plants in need of harvesting?

This is symbolic of soul-level work. For example, if there is a mass of shady overgrown plants that need tending and give a feeling of being choked off (like you can't breathe), that could be an indicator of respiratory problems—either physical, or the body embodying a shadow-work issue. It could be something is blocking your ability to speak up for yourself.

This is the process of observation of your inner space.
What stands out to you?
What needs more investigation?
What might require healing?
Which plant allies are coming forward in this space to aid you?

Everything you are holding on to in your auric body will be energetically displayed for you in your inner sacred grove. This is my preferred way to investigate inner sanctums of self.

It is likely that all the elements of the three realms will be present in your inner sacred grove—water as a river for the realm of Sea, for example, and the air of the realm of Sky above.

Memory in the Inner Sacred Grove

Memory is the currency of life. The memories we create throughout each incarnation are being fed back through the spiritual ecosystem to our original soul. The memories are the point of living, so our soul learns. And nothing is ever forgotten in the spiritual ecosystem.

We are all linked, and we can all tap into the memory of eternity. Memory is the life force that flows through our inner sacred grove.

Journal which of your memories you think have the most importance to you in this lifetime so far—the ones that you just cannot forget or allow to pass into the subconscious memory bank.

Visualize one of these memories, what you remember, any sensory information, and then imagine planting it as a tree, or herb, or flower, or allowing negative hurtful memories to decompose in a compost heap, so that any lessons from it can become nourishment for your future self. You are adding to your inner sacred grove with this process.

Prickly difficult memories might taste bitter or cause us to wince, but it is likely we learned life lessons because of them. If we can plant these lessons in our inner grove, we can utilize the medicine, much like bitter medicine is of great importance across the world.

If a memory is truly hurting us, we need to deconstruct it, allow it to decompose into fertilizer instead. This way we alchemize that negative experience so it is not hurting us as much as it was on a daily basis. (Note, this is alongside needed therapy, counseling, and so forth and is not a replacement.)

We can pop that memory in the compost and pull out anything we think can be planted elsewhere, such as "I survived," or "I was courageous here," or "I learned how this is a red flag for the future." We can visualize each of these parts of memory as a seed to be grown in our internal landscape.

Enriching memories are easy to plant, although it is likely all memories will have a mixture of emotions attached to them because we are human—complex creatures capable of holding multiple views on a situation at once—and memory is an abstract process at best.

Visualization is magic, and with it, you have created a spell. If it is difficult, perhaps allow it to decompose the same way as any other horrible memory, because ultimately, it is real for you.

Finally we have deep soul memory—past/alternative life memory that makes up a part of your personality even though you might not remember that particular lifetime. Déjà vu or innate knowing are two examples of frequently experienced phenomena associated with this—where you feel you have been to a place before, or you have knowledge of something that you can't quite explain.

These are deep-rooted trees in your inner sacred grove. Cherish them.

Casting a Circle: Calling the Four Quarters of Trees in the Sacred Grove

As part of my personal gnosis, I call forth trees in each of the four quarters, after casting a circle and visualizing a sacred grove within. The four quarters is a modern concept whereby each quarter of the circle is associated with an element and a direction. Generally these are believed to be north for Earth, east for Air, south for Fire, and west for Water.

The circle is cast by extending the dominant hand (or a wand/athame if preferred) and visualizing a white line around the self that then begins growing plant life, which unfurls within the sacred boundary as if growing through the floor. A triskele is always found at the center.

For this circle casting, I have utilized the four directional guardians with their relevant element, which includes Fire, not a Celtic realm of existence. In Celtic practice, it is a transitional element, one that is brought forth and extinguished, but as most people will have learned the four corners in circle casting, I have chosen to include it.

There is precedence for this practice as mentioned by Grigory Bondarenko in his Irish mythology when discussing the possibility of the five directions being of significance: "To give an example of the cosmological pentads with closely corresponding functions, one can mention five sacred trees of Ireland as elaborately described in the early Irish place-lore (dindšenchas)."[42] As mentioned before, the five sacred trees of Ireland were Eó Mughna (an oak that bore acorns, apples, and nuts), Eó Rossa (a yew), and Bile Tortan, Craeb Daithi, and Bile or Craeb Uisnig (all three ash).[43] You could use these five sacred trees if you like, but as three of them are ash trees it didn't feel as though it was separate enough energetically.

You can, if you prefer, call in Land, Sea, and Sky, choosing a tree to represent each of them, one tree at the center of each leg on the triskele, or alter which trees are given for each direction.

Each tree has been chosen intuitively for the circle casting, although they each exist within the Celtic Ogham: pine (Ailm), aspen (Eadha), oak (Duir), and willow (Saille).

After the initial circle is cast, visualize it extending above you, and beneath you, in a protective dome of energy, and then call in the four quarters and spirit at the center:

I call forth from the four directions, and the center, the spirits of
  great trees to bear witness to my rite.
I create sanctuary here in this space! I bring forth the sacred! As
  my ancestors did before me, and in the spiritual ecosystem that
  remembers the sacred groves of old.

North,
I call to thee,
Spirits of the northern realm
Where the deep roots dwell in cold earth,
Tendrils of magic yearning,
Fathomless and ancient,
That hallowed crucible,
From which life springs
And the everlasting pine
Grows strong,
Clearing out all that needs to be purified and renewed.
To you I harken well
And beckon thee
To allow me to stay steadfast
'Neath your branches.

East,
I call to thee,
Spirits of the eastern realm
Where the aspen reaches up into the tendrils of wind,
Wrapping ribbons around the branches,
All the memories held.
Your leaves shake and shimmer in the breeze,
Echoing throughout the centuries,
A reminder to speak even when our voices shake,
And sing for those forgotten.
To you I harken well
And beckon thee
To allow me to stay spirited
'Neath your branches.

South,
I call to thee,
Spirits of the southern realm
Where rolled oak leaves shelter,
Forming protective barriers
In Old World canopies.
Rays of light illuminate
Inner chemistry,
The spark that infuses fate
With an indomitable will.
To you I harken well
And beckon thee
To allow me to stay invigorated
'Neath your branches.

West,
I call to thee,
Spirits of the western realm
Where the branches kiss the riverside
And the willow weeps.
The lady heals all wounds, which ache
A song deep into the soul,
A whisper in the twilight realms,
Voices in the rain,
A curtain between veils.
To you I harken well
And beckon thee
To allow me to stay fluid
'Neath your branches.

Spirit, center,
I call to thee,
Spirits of all trees
That connect all worlds,
Formed beyond the common sight,
Unknowable and ancient, come,
Unite us to all that exists and moves,

So that we might be a part instead of apart
Of all that lives.
To you I harken well
And beckon thee
To allow me to stay ethereal
'Neath your branches.

At the center, focus on the triskele beneath you, with you standing at its gateway to the spiritual ecosystem, and see a reflection of the triskele above you.

You are the center between realms. You are the liminal element.

From you, your sacred grove springs forth. I find it is helpful to visualize it as a projection of light and energy that comes from your body and then surrounds you in the sacred space that you have created. The circle is the boundary for it to exist within the mundane world.

Closing Down Sacred Space

When your ritual is complete, you pull the energy back through your cauldrons, so the energy returns to your inner sacred grove and is grounded back within your auric body. Thank the spirits for their assistance, and then situate yourself back into the waking world.

I use the following chant in offering when completing a ritual:

Spirits of (Land/Sea/Sky/Fire/Spirit),
Thank you for your guidance
And your protection
Here this day (or night)
I do not dismiss you,
But I do release you,
May you come and go at your leisure.

(I personally think it is human hubris to "dismiss" spirits—and quite rude, really. As we build relationships with other spirits, we learn that we are a part of this ecosystem, we do not dominate it. The ocean can kill us without blinking. The earth can swallow us whole.)

Then I stretch out my hands to either side of me and call back the energy I sent out, with an energetic pull or retraction, visualizing the energy slowing returning back into my Cauldron of Motion.

I then reconnect a thread of energy upward through the visualized triskele above me (*as above*) and beneath me (*so below*). I finish the energetic exercise with a quick flash of light to signify all the energy has returned to me (*so within*).

I do quite like the Wiccan phrase, "May the circle be open, but ever unbroken." However, if you do not, you can replace it with a statement of closure of your choosing. Then finish with:

All the spirits whom I remember
And who remember me within the spiritual ecosystem,
I honor you.

THE NATURAL WORLD AS SPIRIT WORLD

For a moment, I want you to think about how you visualize the earth in witchcraft or magic, which is so important to hedge witches.

Pagans revere the earth and her bounty, and yet earth magic is equated with being boring (one only has to look at the majority of tarot decks or astrology for this), or there's a disconnect with the deep magics of the earth.

Are we so estranged from nature that we no longer know the depth of its magic? The vitalness of its survival to our own?

I think this is the case.

Humans have ostracized ourselves from nature, with many of us unable to identify plants or trees anymore, with more children able to identify advertising logos than leaf shapes (probably the majority of adults too). We have created concrete and electric jungles, and we have lost much of what it means to be deeply, soul-level connected to the element of Earth. Indeed some people claim that the future is to disconnect from the planet completely and enter an artificial world.

One of the major lessons of earth magic is cyclic living in balance. Without sustenance in balance, something dies. When all works together in an ecosystem, a natural balance occurs. Predators and prey in nature form a equilibrium all their own, with only human interference generally causing problems.

It's not to say all of this is bad—humans work in conservation to preserve life-forms, plant life and animal alike, but this is usually a result of reaction to humans taking too much and being destructive in the past. The Earth too can be harsh, unforgiving, and destructive, albeit not in the same way. Death is simply part of the ongoing cycle in nature.

We must reconnect with the cycles of nature.

EARTH CONNECTION ACTIVITIES

- Document how you feel about your connection to the earth, and what you currently do to try to protect and heal her. Think about what else you might try. Which habits would you change?
- Visualize yourself as a tree, with strong roots going down into the ground. This is a very simple and effective way to ground excess energy into the earth to be recycled. Practice regular grounding with breathing deeply: breathe in and push your excess energy into your roots, breathe out and release.
- Perform a small ritual honoring the earth. Bring a little dirt inside in a bowl, and connect to that by touching it lightly. Speak your truth to the earth, thanking her for all of her bounty.
- Plant seeds in your garden if you can. Make a promise to do more.
- Connect with a land spirit. Go to a place of wildness, a forest, a wood, a cave out in nature, and spend time there. Observe the ecosystem. Observe how you feel. Can you sense a spirit there other than your own? It can be very important to connect to the earth around you, to sense the spirits and what they're trying to communicate to you.
- Set yourself a day when you can spend some time out in local nature and observe. Make notes of what you see, hear, smell, and sense.
- Close your eyes and breathe in deeply in your safe space. Reach out with your senses and see if you can spiritually pick up on anything: colors, a visual in your mind, any kind of communication.
- Express your willingness to communicate with the land spirits, how you want to listen, help, and heal the land. Be persistent! Spirits may take some coaxing.

SPIRIT OFFERING TO NATURE

I recommend creating a land-friendly water offering with herbs and sacred (blessed) water that you can give back to the land. You can bless water yourself by drawing a sacred symbol (such as the triskele) over the top and offering words such as

> Water, I bless you with my breath,
> Water, I bless you with my words.
> Connect to all rivers that flow,
> in spirit and on the earth.

You can then add herbs you have wildcrafted (if possible) or that are in season, creating a herbal water offering.

Place a drawing of the sigil under the bowl and dedicate this spell to the spirits of the land, your ancestors, or all of the above:

> In thanks for the bounty of nature,
> I give back nourishment, in the balance.

I personally add a drop of blood using a sterilized lancet, as it is a part of my life force, connected to the great journey of this incarnation. If you do not feel comfortable with this step, skip it.

You can add any singing, chanting, or dedication to the nature spirits you wish, such as:

> Oh, hear me,
> Spirits of the land,
> Oh, hear me,
> Spirits of all the realms.
> Hear me, in my dedication,
> I honor you this day,
> I give of myself,
> I return to the land,
> Offering in hand.

Take the water outside to a place that is special to you. I lift the bowl above my head and state, "By Sky." Swirl the water in the bowl, "By Sea." And pour the water onto the land, "And by Land," I then hold my hand over my heart. "May this offering bless the land and honor its spirits, and be carried through spirit to my ancestors. And so it was, and so it is. And so it shall be again."

When you think of ancestors, do you immediately think human beings? Consider instead that there is only one kind of DNA, as all animals and plants share the same internal coding for the same amino acids from which proteins are made. The majority of DNA in genetics are the same, respiration is almost universal, and it is mostly mutation that separates us (or evolutionary traits).

Do you feel that spirit connects us deeper than DNA? What does that mean when considering nature and the world part of our ancestry?

THE SACRED ART OF WILDCRAFTING

To wildcraft is to go out into nature in search of its bounty—herbs, roots, flowers, berries, leaves, nuts . . . the list goes on. Witches and herbalists alike go foraging for that which can be consumed, alchemized, or used in spellcraft.

When we engage in this practice as hedge witches, we are even more aware of the life force that is behind every living creature, that each has a spirit, and that which we harvest is giving up either its life or a part of it.

Life force exchange is a key part of what it means to be a hedge witch.

We acknowledge that everything has a spirit, and we are all connected in the spiritual ecosystem, so that when we harvest from nature, we are taking life force from another. This is done with permission only, and with need. We do not overharvest as is done in mass production in the world. Humans' overfarming, overharvesting, and general waste are a scourge on this planet, and we must do what we can (even if it is a little) to address that balance and live by example.

- Take only what you need.
- When approaching a plant, commune with it.
- Practice the art of observation, of being the traveler in its space.
- Be discerning when integrating with the ecosystem in which it resides, pick up rubbish, clear away anything which is not meant to be a part of the natural ecosystem.
- Talk to the plant, introduce yourself. You can be vocal or commune psychically—we are all connected in the spiritual ecosystem, and

other spirits are more receptive than most people realize. They can feel you. Plants communicate in different ways to us—through movement, or sensory impulse, or energetic communication through roots—but they do communicate.
- Be observant of how a plant feels in the psychic sense in response to you attempting to communicate.

You might feel silly at first—that is what social conditioning will do to you. Modern society has a vested interest in presenting the planet as "dead" or at least "brain-dead." The earth is not. She is alive, and all the spirits in her care are too, and they remember. They will remember you, how you behave, how you treat them, if you come with respect and noble intent (or not), and how much you take for yourself.

I always seek to leave life force in exchange. Quite often I will leave a drop of blood or water (connected to the Cauldron of Warming and the realm of Sea), an offering of my breath and of seed for the birds (realm of Sky), and an offering of palm-to-plant touch (realm of Land).

I might also engage in poetic offering, a gift of Awen from my soul to their soul. Songs and poems are long remembered in the spiritual ecosystem, and you can bet it will be sung among the plants themselves, which is a lovely thought.

Plants tend to enjoy being acknowledged and admired. Many will enjoy you drawing or painting them, or creating an offering in writing such as a poem for them (as long as you don't leave a mess behind), because it means that they are remembered. After all, memory is the currency of life, and we all want to be remembered.

If you intuitively feel that a plant is okay with you harvesting it (you will feel psychically uneasy if not), then take what you need with thanks, and leave an offering behind.

HEDGE WITCHES AND THE MORRIGAN

There is no one way of walking a path that is inspired by the hedgerows. The relationship with Pagan gods is an incredibly intimate and personal experience as well, and as such, there are many gods, even under the Celtic pantheons, as well as those of others, that may call to the heart of the witch.

For this section, I write about the goddess who called to me: the Morrigan. I also note that the Morrigan is the goddess to whom I am personally devoted, and as such, my experiences with her are vast.

She is a goddess with an expansive repertoire, but as a hedge witch I recognize that above all she is a shapeshifter, be that through her physical shape, shifting the political and social landscape through war and battle, or through prophecy. As the Phantom Queen, she is also deeply connected to the spirit world.

There are no rules about which deity is best suited for hedge witchcraft, and you may find yourself drawn to others, such as Cerridwen, or Nemetona, or Cernunnos. The spiral path will always be following your heartbeat and your soul cry—you will find what you need on the path of the wild witch.

SOVEREIGNTY AND CELTIC MYTHOLOGY

Within Irish mythology, the welfare of the land itself is directly tied to the person who is ruling it. This is typified by the tale of the heroic figure

Nuada, the first king of the Irish gods, the Tuatha Dé Danann. Considered to be an ideal warrior and king, he led the Tuatha Dé Danann to victory against the Fir Bolg at the First Battle of Moytura on the Plain of Cong, but in doing so, he lost his hand.

In *Cath Maige Tuired* (*The Second Battle of Mag Tuired*), it was stated that: "There was contention regarding the sovereignty of the men of Ireland between the Túatha Dé and their wives, since Núadu was not eligible for kingship after his hand had been cut off."[44]

It was believed that a ruler who was not whole in any sense could not rule (which is an unfortunate ableist part of history) because the land was directly impacted by the ruler, who would have undergone a ceremony to "marry the land": "So it was that the ancient rites of kingship in Ireland included a ceremonial marriage, the banais ríghi, between the king and the goddess of the land, and so fundamental was that idea to the Irish way of life that those rites lasted into the sixteenth century."[45]

Many of the Celtic goddesses are concerned with sovereignty—most of them, in fact—and there are a great many landmarks and rivers named for different female deities. Within Irish mythology, there are several examples of the Morrigan's name being deeply connected to the land itself, to such a degree that she is both the earth and the goddess who represents it.

The Paps of Anu or Paps of Morrigan, near Killarney in County Kerry, Ireland, are of particular significance as they implicate the land itself as the Divine Feminine (that is, the Morrigan): "An equation seems to be made between the body of the goddess and the contours of the earth . . . further suggested by the identification of two of the area's hills as 'Comb and Casket of the Dagda's wife'. . . . The indications are, therefore, that the Mórrígan is identified with the feminized earth."[46]

There are a great many other examples of her name being linked to physical locations, such as the Ross forest known as the "wood of Badb," Inis Badhbha "Badb's island," Gort na Morrígna, the "garden of Morrigan," the Slíab Bogbgna, "Badb's mountain," and Mag Macha, "Macha's plain," among others.

Then there are sites that are not named for the Morrigan but are inextricably linked with her mythology such as the ford at Unshin ("the bed of the couple"), where the Morrigan coupled with the Dagda,[47] and the Ford of Washing where Badb appeared in her guise as the Washer at the Ford, prophesizing death by washing bloody armor, and Oweynagat, which some have mistakenly thought to mean the Cave of Cats, although it has nothing to do with cats—"cath" being the Irish word for "battle" and so it should rightfully be called the battle cave. Indeed it has a long association with the Morrigan, Irish spirit of war and power, who is said to emerge from its depths every Samhain, driving dread beasts before her.[48]

As a hedge witch, I find it of particular interest that the Morrigan is associated with all the realms under Celtic mythology. She has physical locations either named for her or that resonate with her stories in Land (in caves, hills, forests, and plains) and in Sea (particularly rivers and fords as bodies of water, but also for islands surrounded by the ocean). She is considered to be a creature of the Otherworld, and her emergence from Oweynagat is thought to be from the Otherworld. As for the realm of Sky, her most common nonhumanoid appearance is as a crow, with the translation of her name Badb meaning "crow."

Further, not only is the Morrigan a goddess of the land, but she regularly intervenes in the evolving landscape of Ireland by prophesying fate and impacting the flow of events through battle that will lead to a change in rulership. In this form, she is directly impacting the sovereignty over the land.

In the *Cattle Raid of Cooley*, part of the Ulster cycle epic—a legendary Irish text and part of the main mythology of the Irish gods (the Tuatha Dé Danann)—the Morrigan offers to couple with the hero Cú Chulainn. The Morrigan finds her offer rejected and so threatens to hinder the hero instead. During the battle she shapeshifts into a she-wolf, an eel, and a heifer, all three of which Cú Chulainn critically wounds. Following the battle, she appears as an old woman with three wounds and offers the hero three drinks of milk from her cow. He blesses her each time, and each of her wounds heals, much to the hero's chagrin.

Along with her many transformations into a crow, this highlights the Morrigan's role as a shapeshifting goddess, which will be important as part of the hedge witch's path to put on the masks of other spirits to understand their spirit natures.

The act speaks to the otherworldly nature of the goddess Morrigan but also to the impact that Cú Chulainn's refusal had; he insulted not only the Morrigan but the order of the cosmos itself. The story suggests that when the spirit world is ignored—or worse, slighted— there will be consequences in the physical world.

The role of the Morrigan as poetess is perhaps one of my favorite references to her. She says to Cú Chulainn, "Am banchainti-sea em" ("I am a female satirist indeed").[49] We have discussed already the importance of poetry as an energetic force within our world and the inspiration that flows from it when it comes to the connection to the great work of our souls' incarnation in this lifetime.

The examples of the Morrigan changing the course of events and the rulership of Ireland, as well as her power over life and death, are all concepts we can seek to emulate, albeit in a somewhat less grand fashion for the most part! Her tales also highlight the importance of paying attention to the messages that one receives from the Otherworld, because every time she is ignored, catastrophe occurs, whereas when union between the dynamic forces in our universe are achieved, victory occurs.

The coupling of the Morrigan and the Dagda is connected to the Axis Mundi in this fascinating excerpt from Sharon Paice MacLeod: "unite at the sacred portal of Samain, over a river known as the ash-tree, perhaps at the symbolic center of the world or cosmos."[50] She also highlights the importance of the sacred nature of the ash tree (as we saw earlier), noting that it could easily serve as a *bile* (sacred tree at a ritual site) and its association across Europe to the axis mundi or world tree.

I find this concept illuminating because it adds another layer of sacred rite to the union. It is not simply about the coupling of the masculine and feminine, but the unification between cosmic forces, of life and death, of the mundane and the Otherworld, of creation and destruction. As the axis mundi, this would make the Morrigan and the Dagda two parts of the sacred tree through which we travel to other spirit realms.

If this union was also connected to the idea of the sacred ash tree as *bile*, then it adds to the ritualistic nature of the act, and if it is symbolic of the axis mundi, then it infuses cosmic purpose to change the course of events through a central nexus point (or portal) to the whole fabric of existence.

As the change would be wrought on the physical realm, so too would be true in the Otherworld. It is the magical act of witchcraft being birthed from the spiritual ecosystem, a connection among all forces and spirits that sparked a catalyst for the vehicle of sovereignty and legacy that would long be remembered in story and memory.

There are a few interesting references to trees associated with the goddess: "In the wood of Badb, i.e., of the Morrigu, for that is her wood, viz. the land of Ross"[51] and Badb "shames Cú Chulainn into eating dog flesh [that] has been prepared on spits of rowan with poisons and spells. The use of rowan is significant as it is traditionally the tree that protects from sorcery and evil magic."[52]

Forests and trees are particularly sacred within Celtic hedge witchcraft, for they are some of the oldest spirits in our world, and from them the Irish language of the Ogham was formulated.

THE GODDESS MORRIGAN: SHAPESHIFTING

It is my belief that the core of the goddess Morrigan is that of the shapeshifter. While others might call her a goddess of war and death (both of which I believe to be true), it is within her role as a shapeshifter that I believe her true core self is revealed. The Morrigan is change incarnate—she shapes the destiny of the land and shifts the political and social shape of the culture of its people. The land and its ruler are directly tied together in the mythology, and as she holds power to depose a ruler, so she changes the shifting shape of the land.

In the *Dindshenchas*, Poem 49, she is referred to explicitly as a goddess of shapeshifting: "dosrocht ben in Dagda; ba samla día sóach" ("in the early morning the Dagda's wife found her: in this wise came the shape-shifting goddess").[53]

Badb is the aspect most associated with the Phantom Queen element of the Morrigan, showing up in relation to warriors, battle incitement and magic, cursing, and sorcery. Badb is often identified by her voice or in the shapeshifted form of a bird, hence her name, and would have correlated to the very real scavenger crows on the battlefields for the ancient people.

In *Táin Bó Regamna* (the Cattle-Raid of Regamain), Cú Chulainn attacks an old woman driving a heifer from his territory. However, the woman transforms into a raven, and Cú Chulainn, realizing that it is the Morrigan, states that he would have acted more wisely had he known who she was. As punishment for his misbehavior, the Morrigan foretells of her own presence at Cú Chulainn's death in the *Táin Bó Cúailnge*:

Then he saw that she had become a black bird upon a branch near to him. "A dangerous (or magical) woman thou art," said Cuchulain. "Henceforward," said the woman, "this clay-land shall be called dolluid (of evil)," and it has been the Grellach Dolluid ever since. "If only I had known it was you," said Cuchulain, "not thus should we have separated." "What thou hast done," said she, "shall be evil to thee from it." "Thou hast no power against me," said Cuchulain. "I have power indeed," said the woman; "it is at the guarding of thy death that I am; and I shall be," said she.[54]

Later, in the *Táin Bó Cúailgne*, the Morrigan appears once again as a raven (in her guise as a shapeshifter) to warn the Brown Bull of Cooley to flee before Queen Medb of Connact makes her way to Ulster to claim it. With Medb's arrival, the men of Ulster found themselves cursed and unable to fight. Cú Chulainn alone was not cursed and defended Ulster single-handedly.

These are by no means the limits of the Morrigan's shapeshifting, for she has appeared (in the tales we have remaining, at least), as a black bird, a hooded crow, a hag, and the Washer at the Ford, showing that her abilities were not thought by the Irish to be limited to animal form, but it is a popular theme in her mythology.

While it might be possible for the Morrigan as a goddess to perform such an act, there is no act of witchcraft or magic available for the physical transformation (and back) for human beings. The best we have is physical alteration—glamour work, achievable through the materials we wear, makeup, prosthetics or, in extreme cases, surgery. These are shapeshifting of a kind, depending on how retractable they are; if permanent they could be considered more of an "evolution" or "adaptation."

To fixate on the outer physical form is a trapping of our world. Modern society is more obsessed than ever—to a dangerous degree—with what is on the outside. The fixation on what something (or someone) looks like on the outside without due care or attention to what is underneath or within is actually the point of much folklore around shapeshifting. In not recognizing the Morrigan in the beautiful maiden before him, Cú Chulainn failed the test of the goddess and reaped the consequences.

He even failed to recognize her in the hag following the battle in which he had been attacked by three animals synonymous with the Morrigan.

When she appears as an older woman, surreptitiously positioned in the aftermath of a battle with all the same wounds as he had inflicted on the Morrigan, he fails to recognize her again. Instead he accepts three drinks of milk from her, blessing her for each and healing the wounds he himself had inflicted. When he is told afterward, he angrily exclaims that if he had known he never would have healed her!

The point of this is an amalgamation of many parts of my personal practice, which includes how witches—particularly European-based hedge witches—view shapeshifting as a magical or spiritual practice, and how that has evolved in my worship of the Morrigan to include shadow work.

Across cultures, humans who seek a deeper understanding of their spiritual selves often connect with animal spirits. It is key to living as connected to the other spirits within our natural world—ones that many people view as lesser. But the animals within the myths would have been quickly identifiable to those listening to the ancient tales as being the Morrigan. This familiarity (both in the sense of an audience being familiar with the symbolism, and of animals being referred to as familiars) showcases a closeness, a connection, to the goddess herself and the Otherworld.

These animals are by no means lesser creatures (even though the modern hubris of the human condition might suggest that they are!). In fact, the opposite is suggested—that they were divine vessels, intimately connected to the Morrigan, a reflection of her magnificence.

Shapeshifting is thought to be a particularly dangerous magical activity, where one can get lost, lose their way back, damage themselves (and the body to which they are attached) while in soul form, and even cause soul death and/or physical death if they are not careful. This is mirrored in the Morrigan's tale where the old lady version of the goddess has the same injuries as were imparted onto the animal forms.

Shapeshifting Through Shadow:
The Internal Journey with the Morrigan

The first venture into shapeshifting will mirror our external journeys, but because it is within the inner sacred grove, we are within familiar territory. We do not need an external guide, because we are the ground upon which we walk. We may be nervous to stare headlong into our own fears and shadows, with good reason, but if we uphold a sense of self-love, then we will return safely.

Working with internal shapeshifting with the Morrigan is to look at aspects of the self, and for this I have assigned three of her animalistic forms to dominant personality traits, and each of these to a Celtic realm and cauldron.

The three animal forms within the self from the mythology of the Morrigan that we shall be shifting into are the Wolf, the Crow, and the Eel.

The Wolf

- The Wolf personality is associated with the realm of Land, a deep earth energy, and is therefore tied to the Cauldron of Motion in the heart.
- When healthy, the Wolf personality embodies vitality, is personable and reasonable, a team player, and hardworking.
- When in shadow, the Wolf personality is aggressive, beset by anger, territorial, controlling, and even violent.
- It typifies the "fight" response as one of the three major psychological responses to trauma or conflict.

The Crow

- The Crow personality is associated with the realm of Sky and is therefore tied to the Cauldron of Wisdom in the head.
- When healthy, the Crow personality is articulate, intelligent, logical, rational, conversational, and engaging.
- When in shadow, the Crow personality is judgmental, standoffish, cruel, nit-picking, and passive aggressive.
- It typifies the "flight" response as one of the major three psychological responses to trauma or conflict.

The Eel

- The Eel personality is associated with the realm of Sea and is therefore tied to the Cauldron of Warming at the stomach.

- When healthy, the Eel personality is sensitive, intuitive, romantic, poetic, inspirational, and empathetic.
- When in shadow, the Eel becomes slippery with the truth, even to barefaced lying, fearful, isolationist, snappy, and unfeeling.
- It typifies the "freeze" response as one of the major three psychological responses to trauma or conflict.

I could also amend that the shapeshifted form of the Heifer falls under the "fawn" response, often considered the fourth psychological response to trauma, but this would also be in the realm of Land.

It is likely that you have personality traits from all these categories, as the human psyche is far too complex to fit into any one box, but perhaps one is more dominant than the other. You can, of course, be experiencing your shadow through the lens of one of the other personality traits; you mostly identify with Crow, but you have a Wolf response to a particular shadow, for example.

Shadow responses are tied to parts of the self that we disown, or ignore, or repress, and usually come from certain emotional responses that are labeled negatively by society. All emotions are natural and necessary when we cycle through them, but we are taught to label some as bad—anger, jealousy, and fear, for example.

A telling way to identify which shadow we are experiencing is how our body processes it—where do we feel the pain of the emotion or part of self we're trying to repress? Is it causing us gut issues or heartache? Are we mentally overwhelmed?

Once we have made that determination, we can go into a meditative state to meet ourselves within our shadow. We follow the same format as previously described when visualizing entrance into our inner sacred grove, but we alternate which cauldron we enter through energetically, depending on the nature of the shadow.

Shadows of Wolf, Land, Cauldron of Motion

Shadows that fall under this category provoke an emotional overwhelm, such as anger. The shadows may be tied to the body, to do with body image, physical wellness or absence of it, as well as shadows that relate to community and relationships with other people.

These shadows may manifest as heart or chest pain when one feels stressed by them. (Note: Do not ignore ongoing physical symptoms—see a physician.)

Shadows of Crow, Sky, Cauldron of Wisdom

Shadows that fall under this category provoke a mental overwhelm, and because they come rooted in fear, can often cross over with other shadows too. The shadows of Crow/Sky may be tied to the intellect, questioning one's intelligence or capabilities, dealing with imposter syndrome, and overthinking to the point of needing to flee.

These shadows may manifest as tightness in the head or headaches.

Shadows of Eel, Sea, Cauldron of Warming

Shadows that fall under this category provoke an intuitive overwhelm leading to a crisis of self because of emotions we cannot digest, such as jealousy. The Cauldron of Warming is also tied to our sexual self and its healthy expression, and when that is not the case can lead to shadows of internalized shame or self-loathing.

These shadows can manifest as digestive issues.

THE SPIRIT MASK

In the practice of connecting with spirits and crossing the hedge (in all forms), the tool I believe to be of incredible power and benefit is the mask. We shall utilize it when seeking to cross between worlds as well, but when we travel internally, it takes the form of the spirit mask.

It is a common misconception that all masks worn by people in modern society are meant to deceive others. This unfortunate lack of understanding has plagued spiritual circles with the notion that masks are worn to hide soul, that the practice of wearing a mask is not only deception but soulless.

In spiritual circles, the mask should be seen as it is: something Other. The mask belongs on the altar of the witch, in the crane bag of the druid, and in the medicine bag of the shaman. It is an accoutrement of those who shapeshift and seek to understand the Underworld and realms beyond sight, those places viewed only with our other eyes, journeyed to through meditative trance and personal journey work.

A mask is akin to the veil itself—indeed, it is no coincidence that the etymology of veil from the Latin Vela, plural of Velum, is "sail, curtain, covering," and from the Proto-Indo-European root *weg- meaning "to weave a web."[55] When the hedge witch seeks wisdom from their ancestors or gods or other spirits, they seek to pull back the curtain, to glimpse a measure of understanding beyond what we can discern on this physical plane, and further, to discern that great web of interconnectedness that pervades time, matter, and space.

The mask is a physical incarnation of spirit, it can and should be viewed as sacred. By the wearing of different masks, we can learn lessons through the eyes of others, be it ancestors, animal guides, spiritual entities, and even gods. It allows us to think and feel expansively, beyond the scope of our own experiences. Such an instrument can be key in understanding, in empathetic exercises, empowering us with the attributes and wisdom of the mask we have chosen to wear.

The mask is ritualistic. In wearing it, we give life to an action of sacrality. We perform physical acts loaded with spiritual significance, and in this process of transformation we give ourselves over to the energy of otherworldliness. We become what we believe ourselves to be.

To remove the outward expectation that is placed upon us every day is a powerful tool, and not without danger. It can be addictive to step inside a mask and find ourselves transported outside of the confines of who we believe ourselves to be. To step into the spirit realms wearing a mask is described in mythology as being invisible, as journeying to a place and not being discovered by the denizens of whatever realm one has traveled to. This was considered important by those who feared the implications of spirit work.

Such myth suggests that the realm in which we incarnated leaves an imprint on us—identifying us as belonging to this earthly plane. That we can astral travel beyond that is a freedom of soul pathworking, and protection of that soul is often the wearing of a mask.

How ironic it is, then, that such a powerful magical apparatus is dismissed in spiritual memes as being untruthful, when in fact the mask allows us to go beyond a limited form of truth seeking and find something infinitely and expansively worthwhile, so that we might experience the power, lessons, and magic of other beings by wearing different masks.

We will not give in to such fear; we will connect to our primal selves, to the magic within our world, within our sight, that many have forgotten. We will revel in the insight it brings us.

Practice the art of slipping into one of the three spirit masks (Wolf, Crow, or Eel) by entering a meditative state and letting your consciousness travel down through your body into the appropriate cauldron. As you travel through it, you will find yourself in your inner sacred grove at night, and before you is a mask. You will have to put on the mask and allow yourself to express every thought, every emotion, every ugly detail of that personal shadow. Listen to yourself, and journal what comes out, what you visualize, see, feel, and think in that meditation.

You may wish to call upon the Morrigan when partaking of this shapeshifting, as she is the conduit for this kind of shadow work.

CONNECTING WITH THE MORRIGAN AT THE HEDGEROW

For this ritual, there is an assumption of connection with the Morrigan on your part. If you have not been called by the Great Queen, there is the possibility that she will help you in this endeavor (as long as you are respectful), but there is the chance she may not. You can always seek the assistance of other gods or goddesses who shapeshift, such as Cerridwen or Cernunnos. Cernunnos in my experience is the most likely to help those who truly seek communion with the wild spirits of the forests.

For this ritual, it is beneficial to have a physical hedgerow that you can visit. If this is not possible, then create a small altar space that is designed to represent the hedge and provide a physical anchor for the hedgerows in the spiritual ecosystem. Adorn it with wildcrafted local herbs, flowers, or produce from trees.

Remember that we have defined the hedgerow as more than just a physical barrier—it represents a remnant of the ancient woodlands, a border to the realm of spirits, and thus, sacred groves. What might appear as a barrier is a gateway.

This is what is commonly known as "flying the hedge" or "jumping the hedge" as the hedge witch sends their consciousness flying over the border into the realm of spirits. Some will use traditional flying ointments to alter their consciousness and make the visualization process easier (breaking down any physical resistance to seeing the spirit world), which may contribute to the name.

1. Stand in front of the hedgerow (or altar), and relax your mind and body. It can help to close your eyes and then to clench each part of

your body for a count of three seconds and then release with a deep breath, paying attention to the energy that flows into each part of you as you relax.
2. As you relax, allow your body and mind to expand. Each breath should feel deeper, and deeper, as you seek a meditative state that allows the noises and pressures of the physical world to fade into the background.
3. At this stage, call out to the goddess Morrigan:

Hail to the Morrigan in the liminal spaces,
Hail to the Shifter who changes her faces,
Hail to the Carrion to be devoured,
Hail to the maw into which we are loured.

4. Allow your consciousness to drift, seeking the spirit world. Know that you are a spirit as well as human, and you can see with your Other eyes.
5. Quieten your mind of hesitation or suspicion, for today you shall seek to wear the mask of the shapeshifter.

The Morrigan stands before you at the hedgerow, running her long-clawed fingers over the hedge. This is but one entrance to her realm, one of an infinite number.

She is cloaked in black, a long hood covering her entire form, swirling in and out of smoke, of consciousness, of existence. She wears a mask with a corvid shape to it, and holds another in her hands, made of crow feathers that shimmer blue-green in the dusky light. Magic ripples across its surface, and you know that this is no mere adornment but an instrument of change and knowledge.

"Prove yourself," she demands, and the floor is yours.

How you answer will determine the course of events that flow from here, whether or not she will hand you the mask, or deem you not ready. Testing is all a matter of the course.

If she hands you the mask, then put it on.

The visualization I always receive after this point is as follows:

> The Morrigan has changed her shape in front of my eyes, faster than I could blink. She is a war crow, magnificent and enormous, otherworldly.
>
> Her deep crow eyes stare down into mine, and she grows closer and closer, until her beak presses against my nose, and her eyes are millimeters away from my own.
>
> I blink, and at once my consciousness slips away, and I am within the crow, and the crow is within me, and then I fly . . .

And in so doing, the cycle begins.

Pay attention to your surroundings, what the goddess says (or doesn't say), and what you observe. The Otherworld is a realm of tantalizing hints and uncoverable truths. Some riddles will only make sense with hindsight, and some are simply felt with the heart.

TREES AND PLANT SPIRITS OF THE HEDGEROW

There is just *something* about trees.

As a hedge witch I can stare at them for hours, finding them uniquely fascinating, the beauty in their gnarled trunks, the majesty in their boughs. What stories they must have to tell, living as long as they do. How they are infused with folklore with each generation, knowing that we won't survive long without trees.

Trees expand through the realms, deep underground in the earth, and high up into the sky. They exist physically in between, and they create the boundary lines of the sacred groves.

We have seen how they were sacred in Irish mythology, and how a *bile* (sacred, mystical tree) would be the nexus point of ritual sites. Within Irish mythology alone (never mind the mythology from every Celtic area) there is an incredible amount of tree lore, an evolving belief in the magical properties of trees.

As the great creator of worlds J. R. R. Tolkien, author of *The Lord of the Rings*, put it: "I am at home among trees."

The magic of trees is something that has never, to my mind, been in doubt. Their essence is tangible, their presence sovereign, their personalities transcendental; their spirits can be felt and sensed from merely being in their presence.

They are also quite literally woven into the pages of history. They are the vessel for much of the written word, but moreover they are the body for the story of mankind—our history is interwoven with that of trees. As shelters, sacred spaces, written into fable and myth, wheresoever humankind has traveled, the trees inevitably support our existence.

Our mutual lives are symbiotic; we breathe for them, and they breathe for us. Even in an increasingly concrete world, we can seek out the wisdom of trees, feeling instinctively peaceful beneath their boughs, in awe of their looming canopies, and touched by their Otherness.

Kim Taplin, English author and poet, put this beautifully in her studies into literature and ecology: "For these reasons it is natural to feel we might learn wisdom from them [trees], to haunt about them with the idea that if we could only read their silent riddle rightly we should learn some secret vital to our own lives."[56]

It begins as a sort of spiritual muscle memory built into the genetic markers of our bodies. We know without explanation that trees are beyond glorious in their beauty, their energy, their magic. Stories from folklore and mythology wind around their roots, preserving some of the unspoken covenant mankind once held with trees.

This bond survives even as humankind strays further from the natural world. It lives on within our very souls. There are oaths between our kind and theirs spoken by our ancestors and carried through our shared histories. Even though our supposed "rational" minds seek to explain such connection away with notions of human dominance that brand trees simply as fuel, a deep ache stirs within us, and rejects the idea of their lack of sentience, and slowly, scientific discovery supports this intuition.

The first step in this magical awakening is to honor this bond. It is the act of remembering, recalling that trees have always been our allies, for they are our very breath. Without them the entire planet would suffocate and wither, leading to extinction.

The simplest act of kindness is to honor this gift of breath among the local trees, to walk among them, acutely aware of this process. Breathe in, knowing that they sustain you. Breathe out, knowing that you nourish them. This relationship is simple and pure but deeply binding: existence intertwines.

To grow familiar with the personalities and life cycles of local trees, walk among them, sing to them, watch over them. Understand the texture of their bark, the rustle of their leaves, and finally, the shape of the roots wherever visible.

This is tuning yourself to the natural rhythms that are distorted by modern living. Allow yourself to become open to the instinctual feelings that enter your mind when engaging with tree folk.

Take offerings for the trees with whom you interact. Allow your instincts to determine what it is you should give to them. Natural and biodegradable items are far better choices, for this shows an awareness of the natural cycles of growth and decomposition that humans are often apathetic to.

It is highly probable that you will receive recompense for all your efforts as trees give freely of themselves. Any naturally dropped resources that instinctively catch your attention should be wildcrafted and taken away. Branches, bark, leaves, fruits, and nuts are all examples of tree gifts.

When connecting with the archetype or All tree in a meditative state, these resources can be invaluable in helping us to energetically link with the resonance of the tree's vibration, creating a sacred space within the home that opens our internal awareness to the general aesthetic and feeling of each spirit. These physical items provide tactile stimuli that assist the mind to alter its vibrational state and key into the otherworldly vibration behind each tree. We journey to that source of magic by holding the physical keys in our hands and then following that energetic thread via our subconscious.

OGHAM AS GATEWAYS

The Ogham is known as the Druidic alphabet of the trees, originally an ancient alphabet found throughout Britain that is thought to originate in Celtic Ireland, though in modern Pagan practice the alphabet is now used almost solely as a form of divination. The Ogham staves in this practice are cast like runes in order to gain insight into personal queries, and while this can be rewarding to a certain extent within spiritual pathworkings, it lacks the depth of the otherworldly bounty of knowledge that can gleaned by deepening one's relationship with the energies of each tree *behind* the Ogham symbol.

Each Ogham creates a magical and spiritual nexus with the tree to which it belongs; the inscribing and meditative exploration of its runic form is akin to activating an ethereal relationship with the essence of the All tree. The constant association of the energy of each tree with the Ogham symbol that belongs to it over centuries of magical practice creates a bond between them. They create energetic links to our subconscious, much akin to the brain firing neurons and creating new pathways, so that we instinctively tap into an energy source that is both independent of human creation and formulated by it at the same time.

Ogham Meanings for the Modern Hedge Witch

There were originally twenty Ogham associated with trees or shrubs.

Silver birch (Beith): Rebirth, a new cycle, death goddesses, Otherworld travel
Rowan (Luis): Protection and warnings against magic, guardian spirit, gatekeeper to the Otherworld, reveals truth
Alder (Fearn): Defensive magic, keeper of secrets, sustenance for the body
Willow (Saille): Realm of emotions, release, healing
Ash (Nion): World tree, creation of all things, protection, courage
Hawthorn (Huath): Sacrifice, gateway to the Otherworld, vitality and life force
Oak (Duir): Doorway to all realms, strength, grounding, protection
Holly (Tinne): Warrior energy, combat, frenzy, upheaval, prickly situations
Hazel (Coll): Wisdom, wish fulfilment, wisdom, seeking universal information (the mysteries)
Apple (Quert): Love, beauty, restorative qualities, inner strength and healing
Blackberry (Muin): Personal harvests, fruition of plans, fruitfulness, sensuality, fertility
Ivy (Gort): The spiral, search for self, identity, connection to spiritual realms, as above, so below
Broom/reed (Ngetal): Cleansing, purification, a need to change the energetic vibration around you
Blackthorn (Straif): Conflict, arguments, hurdles to be overcome
Elder (Ruis): Love, life, divine inspiration, guards the Otherworld
Silver fir/pine (Ailm): Clear-sighted vision, clarity, breath of fresh air, messages, cleansing

Gorse (Ohn): Protection, fire energy, a need to be careful in a situation, fertility
Heather (Úr): Fae energy, beauty, spiritual enlightenment
Aspen (Eadha): Messages from the gods, fear
Yew (Ioho): Death and endings

Connecting to the All or Sovereign Tree

Each Ogham resonates and embodies the attributes of its associated sovereign tree, and from this vast energetic source boundless lessons of magic and medicine can be gathered and incorporated into our spiritual practices. When we are connecting to the sovereign silver birch, for example, we are linking to the energies of all silver birch that have ever been and perhaps will ever exist within this realm. In so doing, we access the All silver birch energy, or the archetypal knowledge of silver birch.

Journeying to the sovereign or All tree through meditation can be conducted outside while in physical contact with the appropriate tree or by utilizing a substitutional altar space. If neither of these is an option, then the participant is dependent on their own visualization skills.

While it is by no means impossible to create energetic pathways to the All tree through pure visualization, it can impede the journey, for rather than "sensing" the vibrations of the tree at a subconscious level, the active mind can interfere, telling us what we think the tree ought to energetically "feel" like. For most of us, it is not too difficult to come by leaves or twigs from trees by one means or another, and if we lack contact with a particular tree, we can seek out reputable sellers whose harvesting practices align with our own ethics.

The initial stages of shifting our consciousness to connect with the roots of each sovereign tree are based in preparatory work. If you are visiting a tree outside, make sure you are safe and will not be disturbed, that you take a blanket if required, that you have checked the weather beforehand, and so forth. If you are meditating inside, have the ritual space set up before commencing with the meditation, with a comfortable place to sit, music and incense if required, and make sure you will not be disturbed by disconnecting electronic devices.

Consider the reason for connecting with the sovereign tree in question. If you are using meditative music, consider researching appropriate songs beforehand. These are all assistants to ritual, however, and should not prohibit the practitioner from meditation if they cannot be accessed.

Firstly, we shall lay the groundwork with a general meditation template that can be adapted to the theme and tone of each sovereign tree, allowing you to implement your own creativity and experience for each tree spirit.

1. Make sure you are comfortable and free from distraction within your ritual space as much as possible.
2. If you are meditating using a focal point such as a candle, make sure it is anchored and alight. Light any incense you may be using.
3. Wherever possible, place your hands on an element of the tree. If you have access to roots for these meditations, so much the better. Access to bark, branch, or leaf is a suitable substitute. Concentrate on the feel of this plant material, run your fingers over the intricacies, learn the sensation of its touch, the shape and lines of its being, allowing this information to imprint itself into your consciousness.
4. Allow your active mind to loosen while rhythmically touching the plant material. Focusing on your candle or other focal point, absorb the energies of the tree that are imprinted within its roots (or bark or leaves) through your hands.
5. Focus your thought patterns on the principles of healing, the specific type of healing, the root message of this tree, chanting the Ogham's Celtic name if desired and appropriate.
6. Allow your energetic consciousness to fuse with the memory imprint energy from your natural resource. You can visualize this by going inward and seeing your energy as a particular color and that of the tree as another color, allowing them to fuse together, so that your consciousness might travel the spiritual ecosystem with a very specific purpose: to reach the sovereign tree.
7. You may wish to call the tree spirit vocally or speak the name internally within your mind. Speaking the name on any level can help to evoke the spirit of the sovereign tree you are calling on for many reasons. The vibration of the tree is best encapsulated by its name, for throughout the centuries this has been used to summon forth the magical energies associated with the tree.
8. Allow your mind to reach outward. A personal favorite technique is to see a strand of energy unfurl from the self to travel the spiritual

ecosystem. Different practitioners "stretch out" their energy from different points of the body depending on preference. I recommend the Cauldron of Motion as was the case for the inner sacred grove meditation.

9. Allow your energy to follow the energy of the tree that you infused with earlier. Trust in the process as you travel across the roots of the spiritual ecosystem.
10. The process will simultaneously transport you ethereally to the sovereign tree and evoke the sovereign tree before you, which can be a disconcerting experience the first time. It can feel a little disembodying.

There is no shame in practicing the meditation and partaking in the ritual on multiple occasions; in fact, this is advisable in order to deepen your relationship with the sovereign tree and gain further insights.

Following the interaction with the spirit of the tree, document all that you have experienced: feelings, words, sounds, colors, images, vibrations, whatsoever was presented to you. Journaling in this fashion can help structure your magical pathwalking and provide clarity and insights when later dissecting your experience.

Grounding is advisable afterward. Grow your own roots!

THE SPIRIT TREE THAT CONNECTS ALL SPIRITS

As we have discovered, in Celtic mythology (as well as in many other cultures) there is the relationship between the sacred nature of trees and the Otherworld. Depending on which folklore we are examining, there is reference to the axis mundi (world tree) or a specific central ritual tree, the *Bile*.

The idea of one tree at the center of a network is widespread, and it is certainly one I have experienced both at the center of my ritual circles as well as when traveling through the Otherworld. One giant tree that crosses realms, even realities, that phases between a tree of bark and leaves and a bioluminescent creature of light and shadow. It is akin to being the brain stem of the neural network of the spiritual ecosystem.

Being an otherworldly spirit, it can easily shift its shape depending on who is perceiving it. Meditating to find this tree can take practice, but it is such a potent spirit that it is not difficult to find, if a little intimidating!

Close your eyes and meditate on the idea of the axis mundi, perhaps using the (modern) symbol for Koad. This is not an "original" Ogham, but it can still be useful for giving the mind a gateway through which to travel. This Ogham seems to have been introduced by Colin and Liz Murray in their *Celtic Tree Oracle*. It is up to the individual witch whether to adopt this symbol into their practice or perhaps create their own.

Focus on the symbol and imagine it painted on a spirit door, one you can open, and find the All tree behind.

AN EXPLORATION OF ROOTS

Trees and the Ogham associated with them have a deep well of mystical knowledge and wisdom into which the practiced hedge witch can delve, and upon doing so may find themselves awed and somewhat overwhelmed by the sheer volume of information available.

Trees are, in every sense of the word, expansive.

The tree network with the greatest mass, a network of Quaking Aspen (*Populus tremuloides*) growing from a single root system in the Wasatch Mountains of Utah, covers 106 acres and weighs about 6,600 tons (13,200,000 pounds). This clonal system is genetically uniform and acts as a single organism, changing color and shedding leaves in unison.[57]

The interconnection of trees with their natural environment is fascinating on a simply biological level, with the aspen in this "tree network" acting as a unified body via a vast network of roots that relay messages between them. To human eyes, the process by which a system of trees sheds leaves all in the same moments must appear otherworldly—and in a sense, it most certainly is.

The root system of trees is visibly mirrored within human biology; parallels can be drawn to both the neural network in the brain and the arteries in the lungs. While aesthetically similar, they also perform comparable functions: to carry energetic messages and nutrients from one part of the living organism to another to sustain life.

As it is in the physical world, so it is in the spiritual—all life operates interconnectedly and impacts on all life around it.

Therefore, all life on earth forms not only a biological symbiosis but a spiritual one.

We have already discussed how we are bound with trees for the oxygen that we breathe, so it should not come as a surprise as to the synchronicity between the visual makeup of the lungs' arteries to the root system of trees, nor perhaps the neural network within the brain to which oxygen is also vital.

Life interconnects us, and while we can draw many physical conclusions, we must also recognize the spark of life within all sentient life-forms, which has been the conversation piece surrounding human existence and purpose for philosophers and spiritualists alike for centuries.

Spiritual lifeblood flows through the spiritual ecosystem, connecting everything that was, is and shall be, arguably existing outside of the human construct that is time. Many travelers to the astral realms suggest that time is simply a concept of a limited mind creating a framework to simplify their existence, to make sense of a chaotic world.

The efforts of the individual to rekindle the ancient precedent concerning the relationships with trees (and indeed the planet) is arguably vital for the survival of humans. The reconnection with the power and magic of roots is beneficial for the hedge witch, the spiritual ecosystem, and the world. The act of honoring, connecting, and the energetic magical exchange with trees echoes throughout the spiritual plane. As we heal within ourselves, so too do we heal without ourselves.

Roots in generalized terms are similar; they anchor to the earth, they transport energy, impulses, emotions, messages, and nutrients from one part of the being to another, and they interconnect life. For this book, we shall look at a triad of trees from across the hedge: silver birch, hawthorn, and rowan.

SPIRIT OF SILVER BIRCH

Silver birch is traditionally associated with beginnings, given that it is generally accepted to be the first of the Ogham: "On a switch of birch was written the first Ogham inscription in Ireland, namely seven B's, as a warning to Lug son of Ethliu, to wit, 'Thy wife will be seven times carried away from you into fairyland or elsewhere, unless birch be her overseer."[58] It is also associated with the Bardic rank within Druidry where many "begin" their journey. It seems an ideal choice for the first tree to look at within the scope of the Celtic hedge witch. It is commonly around fields and natural hedgerows (sometimes even a physical part of them), marking our first step toward crossing the hedge.

When seeking a deeper relationship with the sovereign energy of each Ogham, however, it is important to go beyond the given meanings, particularly from a modern divination-focused perspective.

The problematic nature of Robert Graves's work *The White Goddess* (from which much of modern Ogham analysis is gleaned) has been well documented numerous times, with the assertion that much of his body of work is not based on evidenced Celtic practice but was assumed or even fabricated by Graves himself (such as in the case of the Celtic trees of the year). "Critical opinion generally holds that Graves was first and foremost a love poet whose poetry dedicated to real-life muses was, to some extent, justified by his loosely academic survey of matriarchal society which he referred to as his 'historical grammar of poetic myth.'"[59]

Many feel that Graves's work is a disservice to an understanding of Celtic history and culture in general. In *Stalking the Goddess,* Mark A. Carter says: "A brief outline of this [Celtic] religion illustrates where Graves departs from commonly known facts and popular opinion."[60] Carter also asserts that Graves's representation of the Ogham is damaging from a historical understanding of what the Ogham originally may have represented and that he even discarded and gave different meanings to certain Ogham so that they aligned with trees.

It is not the primary motivation of this work to be a historical retelling of the origins of Ogham, nor is it the design to insinuate that personal interpretation has no place within spiritual pathworking (indeed, the opposite is true as personal gnosis forms much of the basis of this book). That said, it is important to always question the source material that offers us a supposedly accurate analysis from which to begin our spiritual practice.

This became personally evident when two Ogham initially felt awkward when I was seeking out their energy and meaning—Ngetal and Muin. The given "accepted" meanings of these are reed and vine (grape),

An Exploration of Roots

respectively, however, after further research and spiritual searching, Ngetal is arguably broom in its original form, and muin settled closer to bramble or blackberry in my personal understanding.

Personal analysis of each Ogham is important, as is developing an individual relationship with the energy behind it to connect to the sovereign tree that has become embodied by the Ogham, as well as its shadow.

A general meaning given to silver birch is a tree of "beginnings." This felt underwhelming at best when interacting with the spirit of the White Lady. The impression I received of silver birch was liminal; it felt otherworldly, as though it stalked through the Underworld and absorbed its lessons, Moreover, I always felt the presence of my matron goddess Badb, who is an aspect of the Morrigan.

When spiritually meditating or journeying to the Underworld, it was always the roots of silver birch that facilitated that journey. They would appear whenever there were doors to be entered that pertained to past lives, whenever working with spirits either in a protective capacity or simply to enable communication. Silver birch was also the initiator when creating a spiritual sacred grove in the meditative or astral state.

Initially this seemed at odds with the available material claiming the Ogham Beith to be all about beginnings and not so much the liminal states of being. This led to my tried and tested method of rejecting what I was supposed to be learning from a source or author and to start questioning the intention behind it instead. This and learning to trust the energy I felt when communing with silver birch palm-to-bark, as well as the documentation of my own spiritual journey with silver birch, led me to the conclusion that much was lacking in the divination system of understanding the spirit of the tree.

At the end of what I call the "birch cycle" of lessons learned from this sovereign tree, I happened upon the folklore that supported my personal interpretations. Interestingly, the end of the birch cycle also meant a physical relocation to Scotland at the time, where much of this folklore originated. Synchronicities such as these are usually spiritual indicators of being on the correct path, when messages from the universe all seem to be part of a wider pattern.

There are numerous examples of silver birch (and indeed all trees in the Ogham system) within the folklore from all over the globe, wheresoever those trees can be found growing. The voices of the sovereign trees echo into stories and mythologies across cultures and time, although for the sake of brevity they shall not all be included here! The following are a couple of examples that showcase a relationship with death and arguably with the goddess Badb, who is known for having a spectral phantom element and is also often defined by her banshee-like scream. "The birch has always been associated with the spirits of the dead and with those that mourn, for, in sympathy with the sorrowing, 'weeps the birch of silver bark with long dishevell'd hair.'"[61]

The second example of silver birch referenced here aligns with the themes of death, mourning, and the spirits of the dead. It comes from "The Wife of Usher's Well" ("Of the Scottish Border") in which a mother mourning the loss of her three sons calls forth their restless spirits after not adhering to traditional mourning customs:

It neither grew in syke nor ditch,
Nor yet in ony sheugh;
But at the gates o' Paradise
That birk grew fair eneugh.[62]

For the purposes of identifying the energetic vibration of silver birch, it then becomes necessary to ascertain the energies that best pertain to healing work with silver birch. Common themes that have presented themselves within the energetic nexus of the Ogham Beith for silver birch therefore include:

- The liminal spaces
- Transitional energetic states, including Otherworld journeying and trance states
- Death and spirits
- Communing with ancestors and the dead
- Mourning
- Change as a spiritual concept both in life and with regard to the afterlife
- The goddess Badb within my personal practice (may also pertain to other god and goddess energy with a phantom, shapeshifter, or death aspect)

Silver Birch and Liminality

In all the associated elements of silver birch, each has an energy of being "in between." The liminal spaces speak to being at a threshold or crossing a boundary. It is ideal for the modern Celtic hedge witch.

Journeying to the Otherworld involves transitioning between realms of existence via methods of meditation and trance work. Not only are the realms considered in-between states of reality between what is seen and unseen by the naked eye, but the energetic state of trance and meditation shifts the mind into an elevated vibrational state via altered brain wave activity.

Death is considered by many to be a transitional state, with the human experience entailing many "death cycles" within a lifetime, in which one aspect of life dies off and another is born. Then there is the physical incarnation death. While a full examination as to assert that death is likely transitional would encompass another full book, we can state that all beings in our reality are comprised of energy, and energy never disappears, it simply transcends; thus it would make logical sense that this is the case with human beings. Once we return to the earth, we are once again connected to the planet through the physical and spiritual ecosystem.

With natural transition, blockages to that flow of energy are certain to give rise to ailments, and an identifiable root of personal blockage is of the resistance to change through a fear response. With the mapping of uncharted territory there is always great risk. The forests know just how far humans will go to resist change in many circumstances, and that resistance comes from a place of fear, which is often cemented with deeply negative or hurtful experiences that have resulted from change in the past.

On a personal spiritual level, it can be all too easy to find ourselves in a comfortable space where our basic needs are met but ultimately we do not grow, because we are not pushing ourselves into new and unusual experiences that force us to adapt. Silver birch could arguably be the symbolic tree for adaptation due to the varying climates and lands it can be found in.

Firstly, we must sense this shadow that silver birch raises within our human psyche, and then we must acknowledge where that hinders our personal growth. This is the first step in change, new beginnings, and growth—to adapt our fear response into excitement instead at opportunities. We cannot go backward, in life, in spirituality, in personal and social evolution, because we have already broken through those cocoons of our past selves—they no longer fit.

Shadow lessons concerning fear have us clawing for the old and comfortable, where we know the terrain, the labyrinth is well worn, there is no uncertainty or trepidation. Those answers are all known. But that is a place of decaying husks, where if we remain we allow ourselves to be haunted by ghosts, dictated to by precedent, bounded up in a rigidity that forbids creativity or exploration.

Death is transition and so is life, and the silver birch laden labyrinth within the Underworld led me to a place to bleed my heart and soul into a field within meditation so that I might connect again to the goddess Badb.

Rite of Silver Birch: Honor the Past

The rite of silver birch is designed to honor the past while moving forward in our lives. By creating a symbolic doorway and burning our fears, we create an energetic link between the spell and the behavior within our lives.

Requirements for this rite:

- Silver birch paper and silver ink pen
- Cauldron and matches
- Veil or semitransparent cloth to cover the head
- Ancestor altar or space to honor the ancestors
- Two birch twigs
- Silver birch candle (silver or white) inscribed with Ogham

As previously discussed in preparation for the meditation on each sovereign tree, there are numerous versions of creating an energy of readiness and inclination in which to conduct magic.

Small personal rituals of cleansing can help not only to set the vibration of intention but to disperse distractions of everyday life as well as tune your personal energy into the magical mindset. Cleansing yourself and your space prior to ritual is akin to opening the doorways to magic, and by choosing your preferred cleansing methods you align yourself to the process of personal ascent. This can include a saltwater bath, cleansing with incense smoke, meditational techniques, and so forth.

Set up a personal space to honor your ancestors. Many people choose to use photographs, candles, and incense.

1. Create sacred space.
2. Call to the sovereign spirit of silver birch. Bring forth that energy into your sacred grove space and acknowledge the spirit of the tree.
3. Ask for help in your task: to move through the gateway, beyond any fear responses that are holding you back.
4. Write these fears on the piece of paper, and the responses you have to them, how they are holding you back from the person you wish to be.
5. Cross each sentence out three times.
6. Fold the paper three times, and place it in the cauldron. State the following:

I stand here in the liminal, between worlds,
Between the grove of myself and the grove of the ecosystem,
Seeking a new beginning, with the spirit of silver birch.
As these fears reside in the cauldron,
So they reside in my cauldrons.
I come now to end this cycle, so a new one might begin.

7. Take the piece of paper out of the cauldron, set it on fire with the candle, and pop it back into the cauldron to burn down.
8. Finish the spell with:

May Land ground me,
Sky inspire me,
And Sea restore me.
As it is in the Otherworld,
So it is in this world.
Travel well.

Spend time afterward grounding your energy as you have been taught, in mutual energy exchange. Listen to any messages within the sacred grove from the sovereign silver birch.

Close the space.

SPIRIT OF HAWTHORN

The hedgerow is where the lessons of the hawthorn and the Ogham Huath abound, for once it was known as "haegthorn" by the Anglo-Saxons, meaning hedge-thorn. Within the vibration of hawthorn, many things come to the fore; it has always been an Ogham relating to blood and life force, and as with many thorned plant spirits, it is customary to leave an offering of blood at the hedgerow when engaging with hawthorn. This is a holy exchange, offering up our very essence in a drop at the altar of thorn in exchange for working with the deeper mysteries, crossing the hedge, and gaining access to the Otherworld.

We cannot have personal sanctuary without borders, defenses, and a symbiosis with the natural world around us. For some, hawthorn is merely a lesson in fertility, but its nature goes deeper than that. Fertility within relationships—all relationships, including those with trees—require levels of sacrifice. We must put our honest lifeblood into ventures or they will not succeed. The earth receives our blood as we honor the covenant of the old ways; the hedgerow is one archetype of many that honors the gateway to the liminal worlds, the in-between.

Hawthorn is perhaps the most striking reflection of the complexities of spirit that can be found within humans. Its medicine heals, yet its freshly cut branches smell of death. It is bedecked with beautiful blossoms in May, earning it associations with Beltane and life force, but come autumn its berries and sharp thorns are proudly, fiercely, on display. It reminds us, once again, that we are not separate from trees.

To set up our own personal sanctuaries, this interconnectedness is of pivotal importance. We can learn to tap into the energies all around us and commune with trees in order to weave that energy into our ritual spaces—and what an incredible energetic space the hedgerow is, full of history, culture, echoes of the past when our ancestors cultivated them and shared in their bounty.

When your space is cleansed, create protective borders around it.

There is no shame in being territorial about your space and only allowing that which nourishes your soul into that space. Set thorns along your energetic borders, both physically and ethereally. Tend to them. Remind yourself what is acceptable and necessary within your life, for what you permit will continue.

Hawthorn Spirit Communion

Connecting to the spirit of the plant is an important exercise in wildcrafting, as it builds a relationship to the spirit of the plants (or trees or animals) that you are working with.

Firstly, it can help to use plants/flowers/trees in season (bloom), but it isn't entirely necessary as everything exists within the spiritual ecosystem. The spirit of plants goes beyond the physical realm—same as us. In this case, the spirit would be the "All" hawthorn (Huath), the tree spirit that connects to all hawthorn throughout the spiritual and physical ecosystem, their soul nexus, from which the energy of all plants in our world flows and returns.

Close your eyes and breathe deeply. Relax. Let the mundane world fade away. Use meditative music if that helps. Shift your energy inward, seek the tendril of soul that connects you to the spiritual ecosystem.

Begin by allowing your consciousness to drop into heart space—within yourself. Visualize a labyrinth or spiral at your center, in a bioluminescent shade of turquoise that shifts color. Reach a thread out from the base, down through the body and out into the spiritual ecosystem.

Seek the spirit of hawthorn. Visualize one in your mind's eye, call its name, focus your intention on finding the spirit.

I see hawthorn as an ancient being who has guarded the realm of the gods for generations, knows the wisdom of the crossroads and the potency of wishing. She speaks of sacrifice to gain entrance, of nobility in action and an enduring heart.

From a personal meditation:

"Welcome, traveler, to all thresholds. You have come seeking, but what is it your heart truly covets, I wonder? Speak, and let the petals of your words fly into the winds. Stretch out your palm, and prick your finger on my thorn. Blood is life, and life renews here. It is a sacrifice of your essence for entrance and all the mystery within. Will you take the risk? Is your heart noble?"—Hawthorn spirit

Seek regular communion with spirits to build a relationship with them and ask permission before harvesting for any purpose. The energy you put into these relationships are part of the act of giving back to nature, as your time, attention, and energy are all acts of life force, especially in a world that largely ignores the spirits of plants.

This is a wonderful gift to show the world at Beltane—that you honor and respect the advice of the plant spirits and are willing to be a warrior guardian spirit yourself, for them. Your words, thoughts, and actions *matter*.

Other acts of renewal and rebirth involve discovering what it is the plants need at this time so they can continue their abundance. And as with the sacred thorn that lived in Glastonbury, one of the most famous hawthorns, they may need our activism, our protection. Let us not be silent.

There are many paths to protecting your local wildlife, from political movements to walking the land and offering it your time and energy. Even growing plants and herbs indoors can help protect their line, so their heritage is not lost and their spirits endure.

The hawthorn is intimately tied to the festival of Beltane, it being the maypole, and indeed is sacred to Glastonbury, the spiritual heart of England. Joseph of Arimathea—a prominent biblical figure—was said to arrived at Glastonbury and planted his staff into the land where it grew into the sacred thorn tree. In some versions of the story, Joseph is associated with the Arthurian legends and the Holy Grail—stories thought by many to be rooted in Celtic mythology.

For generations, this hawthorn was revered, and wishes as ribbons were tied in a circle around the tree itself. Sadly in recent times the tree was desecrated, many believe on purpose against the Paganism that resides in Glastonbury.

In Welsh tales, the goddess Olwen, "the flower-bringing golden wheel of summer," was a goddess associated with hawthorn. She was said to have left white petals across the night sky, creating the Milky Way.

In Ireland, many of the hawthorn tales are tied with the Fae, making it one of their sacred trees and very unlucky to cut down. It has become associated with the Otherworld and its entrances, possibly because it flowers around Beltane and berries just before or around Samhain—two sacred Celtic holidays that involve spirits crossing over from the other side.

When hawthorns are found at sacred wells, people often tie ribbons on them for remembrance or wishes. We must be careful with the tradition of tying ribbons to trees as they can suffer from materials being introduced into their habitat. It is possible to get eco-friendly biodegradable ribbon, which should be the ribbon of choice for all crafting regardless, should you wish to engage in this practice. Otherwise, you can either visit local festivals that have a maypole or create a stand-in (such as a candle) and dance at home.

The hawthorn spirit resides between the earth and the Otherworld, and speaks to us of boundaries, guarding our territories but remembering to celebrate our lives at the same time. This energy can help us process difficult emotions with regard to relationships and life force, particularly because it echoes sentiments of the Celtic festival of Beltane. Hawthorn has long been associated with the Fae and respecting spirits within nature that we do not fully understand (even if we seek to as hedge witches). It speaks to us of the Cauldron of Warming, and the vitality that is our heart beating and the importance we place on certain experiences within our lifetime.

Common themes that have presented themselves within the energetic nexus of the Ogham Huath include:

- Vitality, fertility, life force
- Creation and maintaining boundaries in the spirit realms and in the mundane world
- Blood and memory—forming a bond with spirits
- Sacrifice
- The Fae in particular
- Celebrations of life force and nature (Beltane)
- The goddess Olwen

The hawthorn spirit appears as a guardian, all dressed in red. With thorn-made bracelets around her wrist, she stands at the entrance of the hedgerow.

Long has she taught the importance of sacrifice, a little life-blood left in exchange for this knowledge or for the gifts that the hedgerow provides. She has woven ribbons and berries into her hair, and she offers you one now. Something to take with you, to mark your willingness to stand firm with the nature spirits.

Hawthorn spirit speaks:

> Welcome back to the gateway,
> to the crossroad between realms,
> where dirt tracks meet thorned bushes,
> and berries burst in ripeness.

> How far have you traveled?
> Is your heart weary?
> The fight has been long and exhausting.
> We persist. We remain.
> We guard what matters, together.

Your experiences may vary—all are valid! You may wish to ask questions or for hawthorn's blessing when engaging in protection work, revitalizing your weary heart, and creating sacred boundaries.

Rite of Hawthorn: Protection and Boundaries

The ritual of the Ogham Huath/hawthorn is designed to add protection and boundary to our personal space. By creating a symbolic doorway and burning our fears, we create an energetic link between the spell and the behavior within our lives.

Requirements for this rite:

- Red candle inscribed with the Ogham
- Ring of hawthorn thorns
- Pouch and red thread
- Hawthorn berries and spikes (same as the ones in the ring)
- Dandelion root
- Burdock root

As previously discussed in preparation for the meditation on each sovereign tree, there are numerous versions of creating an energy of readiness and inclination in which to conduct magic. Small personal rituals of cleansing can help not only to set the vibration of intention but to disperse with distractions of everyday life as well as to tune your personal energy into the magical mindset.

Cleansing yourself and your space prior to ritual is akin to opening the doorways to magic. By choosing your preferred cleansing methods you align yourself to the process of personal ascent. This can include a saltwater bath, cleansing with incense smoke, meditational techniques, and so forth.

Set up a personal space to honor your ancestors. Many people choose to use photographs, candles, and incense.

An Exploration of Roots

1. Create sacred space as described in the inner sacred grove section.
2. Call to the sovereign spirit of hawthorn.
3. Evoke the goddess Morrigan (or other protective guardian).
4. Bring forth that energy into your sacred grove space, and acknowledge the spirit of the tree.
5. Ask for help in your task: to connect with hawthorn, to create boundaries and safe space so you can heal within it.
6. As you light the candle, petition the sovereign spirit of hawthorn to protect you. State the following:

I stand here in the liminal, between worlds,
between the grove of myself and the grove of the ecosystem,
seeking protection and boundary with the spirit of hawthorn.
From this circle of thorns,
may a wall of thorns surround me and my space.

7. Visualize walls of hawthorn growing around your space. Once the candle has burned down, add the thorns to your pouch—you can add three for the triad or nine (three times three). Then petition each plant spirit of burdock and dandelion as you add these roots to your pouch. Seal the pouch by tying it up or stitching it closed with red threads, which represent the red threads from earlier. State: "May my ancestor spirits protect me."
8. Finish the spell with:

May Land ground me,
Sky inspire me,
and Sea restore me.
As it is in the Otherworld,
so it is in this world.
Travel well.

Spend time afterward grounding your energy as you have been taught, in mutual energy exchange. Listen to any messages within the sacred grove from the sovereign hawthorn or goddess Morrigan.

Close the space.

SPIRIT OF ROWAN

Rowan is well known as the witches' tree, as the berries have a star (pentagram) at the base. An amulet, known as the Witches' Cross, is made by tying two rowan twigs with red thread. Rowan is said to protect witches but also to protect against enchantment caused by witches.

In modern examinations of the energies behind the Ogham Luis, it is almost a universal statement to describe the rowan as "magical," although from that point we diverge into a plethora of folklore, mythology, and the evolution of these threads within the human psyche as to what form that magic takes.

Ivo Dominguez Jr. summarizes rowan in his book *Of Spirits: The Book of Rowan*: "Rowan's true element . . . fire . . . is one manifestation. Rowan has the power to open and to close gates, to summon and to banish, to protect and sustain. . . . All parts of the tree are useful for the making of incense or magical tools."[63]

In the surviving myths and associated histories of the Celtic people of the British Isles, rowan features prominently in all regions and is unanimously associated with magic, although the modern idea that rowan is purely protective against spell casting seems to fall short of the expansive nature of the sovereign tree.

From Irish mythology, the rowan tree is considered to have been brought to the isle by the famous gods of the Tuatha Dé Danann: "Once the Tuatha Dé Danann had played a match with the Féinn and brought from the land of promise crimson nuts, catkin apples, and these fragrant berries, but one of them fell to earth, and from it grew a quicken (rowan) tree, whose berries possessed these virtues [immortality]."[64]

Interestingly, many of the references in Irish mythology refer to rowan with regard to interactions with the gods, as magic was certainly considered a divine trait. In myths where there are seemingly no gods or magic present in a situation, the presence of the rowan tree acts as an indicator that all is not quite what it seems, and usually appears when the heroes of the Irish tales are about to be held to account for their earlier actions. One such myth is in the death of Cú Chulainn in the *Book of Leinster*, where the entire text foreshadows his ultimate demise and his choices that lead to that downfall.

A major event within this saga is where he has to choose to break one of his geis (oaths) by either refusing hospitality or ingesting dog flesh (his namesake as the "Hound of Ulster") at the hands of "three crones" (who in a later version are identified as the goddess Badb):

Then he saw three crones, blind of the left eye, before him on the road. They had cooked on spits of rowan tree a dog with poisons and spells. And one of the things that Cú Chulainn was bound not to do, was going to a cooking-hearth and consuming the food. And another of the things that he must not do, was eating his namesake's flesh. He sped on and was about to pass them, for he knew that they were not there for his good.[65]

In an earlier version of this myth, Cú Chulainn breaks his geis willingly and partakes of the dog flesh, and in the later version the crones stab him with the rowan spit, thus the dog flesh intermingles with his blood and the geis is still broken, with the result being the same. The symbolism of being forced to eat animal flesh that is akin to one's own on an energetic level draws on the very ancient and almost universal taboo of cannibalism. Hooded crows associated with Badb were considered to carry the dead to the Otherworld having ingested them, so the punishment also carries an undertone of a magical removal of some of his life essence and weakening of his spirit.

A geis is a sacred oath sworn by heroes, akin to a magical binding pact with the Celtic gods, and breaking a geis leads to defeat, downfall, and death. The rowan spit is the magical tool by which the "gate" to this fate is implemented upon Cú Chulainn. This tie to enchantment is further consolidated by the mention of "poisons and spells" present in the cooking (alchemy) process, poisons being a tangible version of Badb breaking down Cú Chulainn's spirit.

There are some interesting themes attached to this tale that will appear in other myths involving rowan. Rowan is both a magical apparatus and an indicator that there is something otherworldly about the three crones. This is further emphasized by the mention of being "blind of the left eye," which is another otherworldly hint both in partial blindness and the mention of it being the left side, which corresponds to magic and ritual workings, especially curses.

This ritualized posture appears in other tales of both Badb and Cú Chulainn. In *The Destruction of Dá Derga's Hostel*, Badb as a hag with one eye delivers a hostile prophecy "on one foot" to curse a king into breaking his geis, a posture used by Cú Chulainn as a form of battle magic in *Scéla Mucce Meic Dathó*, which also mentions his utilizing of the Ogham in spellwork: "Then before he [Cú Chulainn] went, he twisted a withe into a ring and wrote an ogham inscription on its peg . . . all with a single hand (. . . with one hand, with one eye closed and standing on one foot). This ritual feat of magic and dexterity, plus the secret ogham inscription."[66] If we are being fanciful, we can draw parallels between the one-legged straight line posture of the ritualized body form and the one-line format of all Ogham.

Rowan is also present in other Celtic myths that involve troublesome magical situations, such as in the folklore surrounding Fionn mac Cumhail, Diarmiud, and Grainne.

In *Bruidhean Chaorthainn* (The Tale of the Hostel of the Quicken [Rowan] Trees), Fionn and his men happen upon a beautiful hostel:

> A fair and beautiful building with bright intricate carvings on the wood of its uprights, and a fresh thatch . . . all around it grew Quicken trees with berries full and red on them . . . no sooner had they entered then . . . the one door was firmly locked. They were trapped. Fionn . . . divined that Midac Mac Lochlan had raised an enchantment against them and was bringing an army to kill them.[67]

Once again, the presence of rowan trees is indicative of enchantment within the story and foreshadow that the protagonists are in real danger. Parallels can also be drawn as Fionn is only released from this spell when his then-champion, Diarmuid, defeats his enemies in battle, beheads them, and sprinkles their blood around the hostel.

It is typical of Celtic mythology that the prospect of binding magic is tied to the blood and arguably the soul of those who cast the spell. A geis is a ritual binding oath that once broken is answered only by a bloody death, and the binding enchantment placed around the hostel is broken only when the blood of the enemies is scattered at its threshold. The mention of the beheading within the myths is of paramount importance as many historians argue for the "cult of the head"—the analysis that ancients Celts believed that the soul resided in the head, given the frequent and

An Exploration of Roots

seemingly sacred references to taking the heads of enemies in battle: "Cú Chulainn beheads them all and he . . . 'planted twelve stones for them in the ground and put a head of each one of them on its stone and also put Ferchú Loingsech's head on its stone.'"[68]

This also highlights the bond between humans and the land, particularly that the blood of the fallen on the battlefield becomes one with the land. Cú Chulainn honors the fallen in death with these stones, even though they behaved dishonorably in the overall tale (attacking all at once when they had sworn not to do so), and the land is then named Cinnit Ferchon in remembrance of the battle instigated by Ferchú Loingsech.

The connections between the rowan tree, enchantment, betrayals, and beheading can be seen again in the later stories of Fionn and Diarmuid, this time with Diarmuid absconding with Grainne, Fionn's betrothed. Fionn offers a truce to his former enemies, the Mac Mornas, if they retrieve either Diarmuid's head or a handful of quicken (rowan) berries from an enchanted tree—the same tree, as Irish mythological deus ex machina would have it, that a pregnant Grainne desired the berries from to eat. So Diarmuid killed its protector (a giant) so that she might sate her cravings. The army arrives, and a peculiar game of chess ensues which proves that Diarmuid is hiding in the tree, but he escapes by leaping over the heads of the Fianna, leaving Grainne, who is later rescued by Óengus Óg, the Irish god of love.

Once again, a rowan tree is rooted around the concept of revealing what is hidden—this time the tree itself is noted as being enchanted or magical, further cementing the otherworldliness of this particular tree, whose myths tie it to the realm of gods, spirits, the Otherworld, and the practicing of enchantments.

Common themes that have presented themselves within the energetic nexus of the Ogham Luis for rowan therefore include:

- Rowan as indicator of a casting of enchantments both benevolent and malicious
- Rowan present particularly within binding rites that hold individuals to account for their actions
- Rowan revealing the truth of a situation
- Rowan being magical within its own being—a tree spirit akin to the magician archetype

- Rowan as a gatekeeper with emphasis on the opening and closing of those gates

A Note on the Use of Spells

In realizing the shadow aspect of the rowan tree and the lessons of the sovereign energy behind the Ogham Luis, we must consider the human relationship to the concept and utilization of magic.

Regardless of the debates around ethics and spell casting, the choice of how to utilize magic is a decision made by (and answerable to) only the practitioner themselves. The spells associated with rowan in Celtic mythology highlight how magic can be used to capture others against their will, lead others to harm, deceive and even kill others.

Human beings have a natural tendency to seek all methods through which to control their lives, their environment, and even other people. Magic and ritual can easily be viewed as another technique by which this dominance can be asserted, especially as a large section of society are apathetic toward the esoteric traditions, forgetting the wisdom of their ancestors.

Feelings of subservience are thus often problematic in modern societies where self-sufficiency is a minimum requirement of acceptable social standing. What this societal standard means is subjective, changing from person to person, so that an individual determines their own ideals of independence. This creation of an ideal based on values disconnected from a sense of community and even the value of unique traits can easily lead to a person poisoning their mind and thus their reality if their personal power is undermined.

In the myths concerning Fionn, despite him having magical ability himself, he finds his authority betrayed on multiple occasions. The enchantments in the mythology are symbolic of challenges to Fionn's sovereignty by those wishing to usurp him, both as a ruler and a husband. Fionn demands violent retribution or a magical boon in the form of rowan berries as recompense for these slights.

Magic is therefore by definition a system of affecting the world around us to our benefit, and that benefit hinges on the will of the practitioner, their reasoning, their emotional state, and their self-justifications.

Magic can certainly be used to empower the self, but by the same token it can be utilized to disempower, whether that act is aggressively toward a perceived enemy or unwittingly against the self in a self-perpetuated form of binding or curse, not unlike the symbolism present when Cú Chulainn is portrayed ingesting dog flesh.

The strongest and most debilitating curse is when the practitioner believes themselves to be cursed and/or deserving of that curse. Not only will their belief manifest itself through the conviction placed in this perception but the energy they place behind every emotion in reaction to this view and behind any behavior that stems from it. It becomes an intentional act and consequently a magical one.

In these ways and others besides, the irrational beliefs and responses of a practitioner can place their personal power in the hands of other people, leaving them bereft of the emotional security of self-ownership. In the absence of their personal power, humans frequently seek to dominate and control other people or their environment in a largely futile attempt to regain lost authority.

Then there are figures of authority within our lives who seek to supplant our freedom to perform magic itself. This has been an issue throughout history and remains so today. One of the most affluent witch hunters in British history was King James I, who in his *Daemonologie* of 1591 sought to condemn "such kinde of charmes as commonlie dafte wives uses . . . by knitting Roun-trees or sundriest kinde of herbes, to the haire or tailes of the goodes."[69]

Not only does this historical example condemn witchcraft from the monarchy—which was the most powerful role within the system of government at the time—it also draws attention to a charm made of rowan.

The rowan tree cross is said to originate in Scotland, with a museum receiving one in 1893 though the charm itself was dated as much older than that. Examples of rowan being used to counter magic abound within history surviving in folklore and song:

> The spells were vain; the hags returned
> To the queen in sorrowful mood,
> Crying that witches have no power
> Where there is rown-tree wood.[70]

Another example of people seeking to nullify the magical powers of others using rowan comes from the classic study of magic and religion *The Golden Bough*: "The people believed that on that evening and night the witches were abroad and busy casting spells on cattle and stealing cows' milk, to counteract their machinations pieces of rowan tree . . . were placed over the doors."[71]

Both rowan and the action of spell casting are therefore available to everyone, removing the idea of exclusivity of this type of power. While proficiency at spellwork can be (and vehemently is) debated as a form of power play, it gives rise to the shadow of the rowan tree—a feeling of absence of the value of uniqueness and the knowledge that superiority is a fallacy. There are no real kings and queens in modern Western society, only figureheads—empty vassals who cling to the remnants of real power.

Today, the rowan cross survives as testament to its power over the hearts and minds of magical folk. It is just as famous and popular with witches and the like as a folk charm of protection as it ever was, despite attempts to demonize or trivialize it. In many cases, the power of the Ogham Luis is added to the charm to draw power from the sovereign rowan and bolster the protection enchantment.

It is interesting that the power of rowan/Luis survives within the skill set of folklore and the cunningfolk who harmonize with the energies of the land. Just as Cú Chulainn honored the relationship between the fallen and the earth with standing stones, it seems clear that where power really lies is in the energy and harmonization with said energies of the land and its spirits.

To utilize the shadows presented by rowan energy, we simply acknowledge and work alongside the power present with its spirit. This could be considered a moment of surrender on the path to true power, the realization that there are many spirits in this world outside of the mundane realm of human beings that are just as powerful, if not more so, than people.

Let us discard the modern conceit of land "ownership," for it seems a far stronger position to be a guardian of the land, one who listens to the lessons of plant and tree spirits, who honors that connection and works tirelessly to get back in touch with a natural rhythmic and cyclic life. Mastery over other people is similarly an illusion, for people will always resist that control, especially if they are aware of the detriment to their lives or well-being. The human spirit could even be defined by its resilience to oppression as new dictators inevitably rise to try and assert their brand of control. These moments of power are—in the grand scheme of the universe—fleeting blips with grave consequences. A broken geis by a ruler ignoring their duty to their people and their land is always answered in blood and death.

Those who seek to govern the land might refuse to remember their sacred duty to it, might ignore their bond to the earth and the deva spirits all around them, but the land does not, and nor do the entities attached to it. Self-serving arrogance without honor is a broken pact and the payment will always come due.

Pollution of both the land and the self are highly problematic acts that stem from the shadow of the rowan, and the lesson here is remembering that we too were born from a womb of the earth, we are sustained by the earth, and one day, our bodies will return to it. We are connected, enriched, and sustained when we work with the spirits of the land.

Ritual of Rowan: A Pact of Blood to Bind the Corrupt

The ritual of the Ogham Luis/rowan is designed to create a bond with the land in order to topple a mutual enemy who has harmed yourself and the local spirits. As we have already seen, corrupt rulers or leaders fall into this category as they have, probably unwittingly, broken their geis to protect the earth.

This spellwork is all the more potent if the individual has caused physical damage to local wildlife—if they ignore the illegal fox hunts to profit from the wealthy, if they tear down and pollute the woods to line their own pockets, if they evict vulnerable tenants on a power trip—then the spellwork will be further bolstered by agitated land spirits.

The magical pact for rowan will energetically tie you to the land spirits and officiate you as a spokesperson for the sovereign spirit of rowan, which as we have discovered, is particularly concerned with the magical arts.

Honoring this relationship is of tantamount importance, as following the ritual the magician can keep deepening their energetic symbiosis to the sovereign rowan and the land spirits around them, gaining access to all forms of magical knowledge and forgotten wisdom. For the purpose of the "pact of blood to bind the corrupt," becoming a guardian of the rowan tree enables the magician to speak to the affront of behaviors of the corrupt, on their behalf, as well of the land and tree spirits.

Requirements for this rite:

- Access to your own blood through a clean sterilized method; a medicinal lancet is recommended or women can utilize their menstrual blood.
- An area of local earth where you can commune with the spirits of the land, ideally with a rowan tree within the space. If this land has been damaged by the corrupt in some fashion it will also bolster the magic.
- Altar or shrine space to privately continue the ritual dedicated to the rowan spirit.

Prior to the ritual:

As previously discussed in preparation for the meditation on each sovereign tree, there are numerous versions of creating an energy of readiness and inclination in which to conduct magic.

Small personal rituals of cleansing can help not only to set the vibration of intention, but to disperse distractions of everyday life as well as tune your personal energy into the magical mindset. Cleansing yourself and your space prior to ritual is akin to opening the doorways to magic, and by choosing your preferred cleansing methods you align yourself to the process of personal ascent. This can include a saltwater bath, cleansing with incense smoke, meditational techniques, and so forth.

Set up a personal space to honor your ancestors. Many people choose to use photographs, candles, and incense.

1. Create sacred space as described in the inner sacred grove section.
2. Call to the sovereign spirit of rowan.
3. Evoke the goddess Morrigan (or other protective guardian).
4. Bring forth that energy into your sacred grove space, and acknowledge the spirit of the tree.
5. Ask for help in your task: to protect the spirits of the land from oppressors.
6. Exchange a drop of blood with the land, calling forth the rowan tree spirits as guardians.

7. Take some of the rowan back to your altar space, such as berries, leaves, or twigs.
8. Call the spirits once again at the altar. State the following:

I stand here in the liminal, between worlds,
Between the grove of myself and the grove of the ecosystem,
Seeking protection and boundary, with the spirit of rowan.
I have bled for the land to connect deeply to it,
I honor the land from this day forward.

You may wish to make a protective rowan cross as described above, to protect you from harmful spells and to protect the land as well.

9. Finish the spell with:

May Land ground me,
Sky inspire me,
And Sea restore me.
As it is in the Otherworld,
So it is in this world.
Travel well.

Spend time afterward grounding your energy as you have been taught, in mutual energy exchange. Listen to any messages within the sacred grove from the sovereign rowan or goddess Morrigan.

Close the space.

TREES AS GUARDIAN SPIRITS

If you have partaken in these rituals or spirit work within your internal sacred grove, then you have begun forming relationships with tree spirits. You have connected to the sovereign or All spirit of silver birch, hawthorn, and rowan, all chosen because they are protective spirits that will assist you going forward in your journeys through the spirit realm.

You can further your relationship to these spirits (and indeed those present in the Ogham) by connecting to them regularly. You can craft your own Ogham set for divination purposes by collecting a small branch of each wood and using pyrography (woodburning) to add the symbol for each tree or just paint it on. Then you can pull a daily Ogham (or weekly if you prefer) and make notes about your experiences.

If you are able, seek out each of the trees in the wild and sit with them. See if you can intuit any energy coming from the tree—although it might take many trips to build up an energetic bond. Much like people, spirits require patience and the forming of a bond. You could take natural offerings, seeds for the birds, water, or a simple offering of words or song (Awen).

You can also make room in your internal sacred grove for one of each of these trees and make it a regular practice to visit them in meditation. The more you practice this, the easier it will be to communicate with the spirits of each tree.

Trees tend to be open to witch interaction, if they have not been harmed by humans. They are natural guardians, and they span through the different realms, connected to Land, Sea, and Sky, which make them an incredible spirit ally for the hedge witch.

A tree spirit as a guardian when traveling through the Other realms is invaluable—as all sovereign tree spirits connect back to the axis mundi, the world tree at the center of the spiritual ecosystem. If you are in difficulty when partaking in spirit travel, a tree spirit who has agreed to assist you will always be able to bring you back to yourself quickly.

NON-OGHAM PLANT SPIRITS

There are a few plant spirits of the hedge that I believe every hedge witch should seek out, both in terms of wild harvesting and in connecting to their spirits. To begin your journey I have included bindweed, nettle, and dandelion.

Bindweed

Bindweed is a hedgerow plant with strong spiritual medicine that is treated as a pest because it, like other vines, can spread and destroy the cultivated gardens of people. Bindweed belongs to the liminal energies and magics; being of the hedgerow it is associated with times of the in-between, of dusk, twilight, and also dawn, where all possibilities lay present.

It is a plant that gives itself to the Otherworld, a gatekeeper that roots itself deeply in the hedge. Its tenacious vines and roots create both a connection to and a bridge between the realm of the Other, making it invaluable to spirit workers and hedge-riding witches. This connection means that one can easily keep the door open and travel safely back from the Otherworld.

Bindweed grows counterclockwise and is ruled by Saturn, who also governs witchcraft, and would be an ideal herb to honor the goddess Badb. The anticlockwise growth as well as being a vine that can choke the life out of other plants if left untended means that bindweed also lends itself to binding work and curse work. Destructive magic can also destroy situations that just won't seem to end; bindweed can break a situation down so that one might start again.

Magical Properties of Bindweed

- Substitute for High John the Conqueror root—good luck, success, self-belief, strength, commanding power
- Journeying, shamanic opening of self, hedge-crossing
- Bridge to the Otherworld
- Binding and cursing
- Destructive magic
- Holding someone to a contract (magical or otherwise)

The hedge witch should definitely make use of bindweed and its spirit when seeking to be safe traveling in between worlds. A tether made of bindweed is a safety rope to connect you to this world, as its tenacious spirit understands not only how to open you up to the Otherworld but how to tenaciously refuse to surrender to dangerous or difficult circumstances.

Other than local names for bindweed, it seems its folklore is sadly absent.

Connecting to Bindweed

Close your eyes and breathe deeply. Relax. Let the mundane world fade away. Use meditative music if that helps.

Shift your energy inward, seek the tendril of soul that connects you to the spiritual ecosystem.

Begin by allowing your consciousness to drop into heart space—within yourself. Visualize a glowing red heartbeat that becomes a thread, which travels down and becomes one with your Cauldron of Motion, and the light traveling down through your body into the earth.

Connect with the spiritual ecosystem at your base, in what some call the root chakra or the (spirit) womb cauldron. You can also spread your roots through your feet energy centers.

Allow the energy of the spiritual ecosystem to rise through the earth and mesh together with your thread in mutual exchange or balance. Roots seek roots. They interweave throughout the ecosystem and create a network—a spiritual root system.

Seek the spirit of bindweed. Visualize the plant in your mind's eye, call its name, focus your intention on finding the spirit.

Hear or speak the words:

We call out across the spiritual ecosystem, seeking the All spirit, the great spirit, of bindweed.
That nexus spirit which connects all like plants together, sharing their memories, experiences, and wisdom. The tenacious conquering vine.
We wish to connect to this magic.
We call out, in song, to them:
Come, come, come, bindweed,
That tangles through the hedge
Come, plant spirit that conquers all,
Come, come forth

Come, come, come, bindweed,
That tangles through the hedge
Come, plant spirit that creates a bridge,
Come, come forth

Come, come, come bindweed,
That tangles through the hedge
Come, plant spirit that opens the soul,
Come, come forth

Visualization

As you open your Other eyes, find yourself on the edge of an ancient hedgerow by a well-worn dirt-track road. The hedge is teaming with life, spiked thorns, red berries, birds that flit in and out to feed their young. You stand on the dirt path admiring it, viewing the full length of the hedge, and walk along it.

At the end of the hedge is a ditch full of bindweed, crawling and tumbling along the floor, rambunctious, hated by many, its curved vines weaving in and out of existence, its white flowers like trumpets blowing in defiance.

The weaving of the vines has created a kind of doorway, a hole in the ditch at the center, as though the plant has encircled a burrow entrance, and nothing but darkness can be seen within it.

The bindweed circles it, dances around it, whispers to it.

This is an entrance way to the Otherworld.

Bindweed has all the secret knowledge of the liminal curled within itself, a wisdom so ignored because it is so judged. It is not cultivated or prim; bindweed refuses to be proper and fit into the laws of the human gardener. It will take and take and drain this mockery of nature, given half the chance.

But you are here in the capacity as witch, and bindweed knows this and responds, letting you see the entrance, a dark pool of air that whispers, between Land and Sky.

You steady yourself, feeling nervous at the sight of light within the portal, readying yourself for the journey.

You breathe in, and out.

You breathe in, and out.

You breathe in, and out.

You step forward and can almost hear the plant breathing, waiting to see what you will do. Interested to know if you can cast off the shackles of perception and see beyond what mortals see.

If you can connect with the purpose, the magic, and lay down your preconceptions.

You ground into the space, feeling the earth beneath you as anchor and the air all around tugging at your hair.

You step forward, and bend down, lowering yourself into the burrow space, climbing deeper and deeper into the earth, letting only your hands guide you.

Carefully, steadily, each placement of your feet measured.

At the bottom is a deep cavernous space, and as you step into it, something shifts—your eyes adjust, and you see—a spiral beneath you, and a spirit before you.

The spirit of bindweed—a tangled movement of vines and flowers, devastating and beautiful, strong and resilient, proud.

The movement of the vines does not stop, instead shifting around the general shape, with two glowing eyes watching you, beckoning you forward to speak.

> Bindweed spirit speaks:
> It is a rare and precious thing
> For a witch to visit me here,
> For I am so often ignored or treated with malice
> Simply for existing
> And I have carved out my existence
> Inch by inch by inch
> Letting my claws go deep even as they come with fire
> With chemicals
> Burning my skin
> Yet you have sought me out
> Interested in all the things I might know
> That I might share
> And protection too, if you're worthy.
> Yes, I see. I could be persuaded.
> I do so love traveling the realms,
> Doing things they only dream about,
> And if they would speak with me kindly,
> Would know. You will know these secrets. . .

Sit with these words for a while. See how they make you feel.

When you are ready, give thanks to the spirits of the bindweed. You may wish to give an offering of blood or breath (in the spirit world). You can sing or speak words of gratitude.

You may wish to drink a libation such as tea or water. See how it makes you feel after doing so and journal that experience too.

Then bow (out of respect), and come back the way you came, up through the burrow, and out of the hedge. With each step, reconnect back to the earth, grounding off the excess energy. Grounding back into our world.

Open your eyes and come back to yourself.

Nettle

Nettle is written into history as shown by a recording of an ancient Anglo-Saxon healing charm:

> Nettle it is called, it attacks against poison,
> it drives out the hostile one, it casts out poison.
> This is the herb that fought against the serpent,
> it has power against poison, it has power against infection,
> it has power against the loathsome foe roving through the land.[72]

Nettle is often ignored as a weed or a nuisance when in fact it is a plant with incredible healing powers and alternative uses. It can be made into revitalizing tonics, herbal tea for a wide range of healing effects, and braided into twine. It is also a reputed hemostatic (limits blood flow) in poultices, can be made into soups and salads, and all of this before any metaphysical qualities are examined.

Nettle can nourish every part of the body and soul, but in modern times its magic, much like dandelion's, is ignored and written off as a weed that stings. Perception is skewed as mankind drifts away from the voices of nature; the plant devas' calls often fall on deaf ears. It is the course of the herbalist, the spiritualist, the witch to remind the world that magic exists, that the lessons plants have to tell us (or remind us) are of paramount importance.

Nettle is a plant that stings if you are not careful, but treated well, carefully harvested with respect and honor, it becomes a stout ally, blending magic and medicine into one seamless energy. Helpful, dependable, and courageous, nettle will not allow itself to be mistreated. Grab it ruthlessly by the hand and you will find yourself stung.

It is a lesson on grace and understanding, to look for the internal problems of "grabby hands." We should not always be taking but seeking to maintain a balance, a relationship. The earth is not a resource to be used or drained; she is alive, to be nurtured, cared for, cultivated, harvested, and honored.

Human beings should be the caretakers of this great garden, not its destroyers.

The same is true for the garden of your heart, mind, and soul. You must cultivate it, prune the hedgerows, plant the flowers. When mud is slung at you, plant flowers in it. Feed your garden with all those energies it takes to help you blossom, and blossom you will. Tears are the rain that dampens, laughter is the light that helps it grow—all these things are necessary and more. You must take care of yourself. Do not let poisonous vines take hold of your life, cut them down and cleanse the soil. Plant the healers. Honor those within your life who honor you.

On the surface, nettle is not a showy plant. It doesn't have extreme color variation or a blossom scent, and people dismiss it as prickly. Their shallowness betrays them, for nettle has more than they can see—such depth, such promise, such magic to weave . . . a plant for the soul.

Magical Properties of Nettle

- Protection
- Take the sting out of someone (make them less antagonistic)
- Consecration and deep cleansing
- Can be made into thread/yarn and used in knot magic or for witch ladders
- Roots are extra protective and can be used in money magic (paired with alum they create a gold dye)

Connecting to Nettle

Follow the instructions from the Bindweed meditation.
    Hear or speak the words:

> We call out across the spiritual ecosystem, seeking the All spirit, the great spirit, of nettle.
> That nexus spirit which connects all like plants together, sharing their memories, experiences, and wisdom. The weaver of spirit.
> We wish to connect to this magic.
> We call out, in song, to them:
> Come, come, come, nettle,
> That stings and heals at once
> Come, plant spirit that protects,
> Come, come forth
>
> Come, come, come, nettle,
> That stings and heals at once

Come, plant spirit that creates thread,
Come, come forth

Come, come, come, nettle,
That stings and heals at once
Come, plant spirit that makes sacred,
Come, come forth

Visualization

As you open your Other eyes, find yourself on the edge of an ancient forest, where the trees are gnarled and thick, the canopies are deepest emerald green, and the scent of the ancient world fills your senses.

It is a place of old, untouched beauty, where nature creates a cathedral all by herself without interference. Where animals roam freely, unbothered by humans. Where the insects flit in between the branches, their wings beating fast as they're chased by black winged birds.

The forest space connects you deeply to a wildness within yourself, and you look up, admiring all that is above you, forgetting to watch your step as you pace into the depths.

And you feel a sting right in your thigh.

You were careless and did not pay attention to the earth, stepping on a nettle, and its brother will have recompense.

The sting is familiar—you know it from your childhood when you were wild and free, running through fields without looking.

You apologize to the nettles, taking a step back. Fortunately you did not cause much harm with your feet, and you get the sense that your apology was . . . unexpected.

The forest seems to hold its breath.

You take a step back, and sit cross-legged on the grass, a small distance away from the nettles and the forest itself. You can feel the realm of Land within that forest, and know that nettle is a guardian. Whether a guardian for the realm, or for you, or both . . . you are not quite sure yet.

You nod your head, and ask to speak to the spirit of the nettle.

You breathe in, and out.

You breathe in, and out.

You breathe in, and out.

You focus on the nettles now, their longer than usual stems thick and healthy, covered in all those barbarous little hairs, ready to strike. The thick, lush green leaves bobbing in the breeze, not content to be still but ever moving, watchful.

You send out a silent request once more, saying that you meant no harm, although you may have been overexcited to investigate the forest, so once again you're sorry if you squashed anyone.

You feel your senses grow thicker, like a filmy layer descends, as the spirits connect back to you, a tendril of consciousness reaching out, silvery green, across the space. You allow yourself to drift, and see the spirit of the nettle willing to speak—appearing like a small Fae creature, not quite solid in appearance, flitting and full of movement, with sharp teeth should it need them.

Nettle spirit speaks:

We are the weavers and the healers,

The warriors with bite,

And if you try to harm us

You're in for such a fight.

But if you come in friendship

And don't mean any harm,

Then the gifts we offer

Can be quite the balm.

We work in communion,

An ecology we bring,

And when you care to listen

You will find we sing.

Sit with these words for a while. See how they make you feel.

When you are ready, give thanks to the spirit of the nettle.

You may wish to give an offering of blood or breath (in the spirit world). You can sing or speak words of gratitude. You may wish to drink a libation, such as nettle tea. See how it makes you feel after doing so and journal that experience too.

Then bow (out of respect), and come back the way you came. With each step, reconnect back to the earth, grounding off the excess energy. Grounding back into our world.

Open your eyes and come back to yourself.

Dandelion

Dandelion is one of my favorite plant spirits to work with as a witch. Its power has been maligned, I believe, in favor of pharmaceutical culture and systematic oppression of herbalism and the healing it brings. I put my Gimli voice on and cry, "And they call it a weed! A weed!"

Dandelion is pure magic. Its essence is resilient, determined, unbreakable. It will thrive wheresoever it sets its mind to and pays little attention to humans and their ridiculous anti-ecology lawns. It feeds the bees, and in medicine and witchcraft, it is a full-course feast of spiritual purpose.

> The first recorded information about dandelion comes from Roman times. Use has been noted by the Anglo-Saxon tribes of Britain and the Normans of France as well. In the tenth and eleventh centuries there was mention of dandelions used for medicinal purposes in the works of Arabian physicians. All in all dandelion has been a well-loved, well used and well-traveled plant.[73]

All parts of the dandelion are edible leaves, flowers, and roots. Dandelions are a good source of vitamin A, vitamin C, vitamin K, and vitamin D, along with calcium, iron, magnesium, and potassium. Dandelion can be used in salads and teas, the root is used as a coffee substitute, the flowers are added to cakes, infused into honeys and wines, they can even be pickled.

Its medicinal uses are vast too: it acts as a mild appetite stimulant, improves the digestion, boosts the immune system, provides antioxidants, is good for the skin, and is said to cleanse the blood and liver. What a super plant!

In Greek mythology, it is said that Theseus ate dandelions for thirty nights in preparation to fight the minotaur. Dandelion are called "fairy clocks" because their flowers open and close predictably. Dandelion is used as a tool for divination. If you blow a seed head, the number of seeds remaining are the number of children you will have.

It magically corresponds to Jupiter, although some link it to the sun. It is said to correspond to the element of Air and the zodiac signs Sagittarius and Pisces. Dandelions are said to be sacred to Hecate. This seems to be a universal idea although its foundation is vague as to why this is.

Dandelion bleeds a cloudy sap, possibly referred to in *The Root-Cutters* by Sophocles: "Medea receives the juice whitely clouded, oozing from the cutting." Dandelion is a plant of the Underworld and summoning spirits of all kinds, and is used to enhance psychic ability, opening the psychic senses to messages from the Other side. This element may also have led to some of the hostility toward it—the plant is inherently witchy!

Magical Properties of Dandelion

- Spirit communication
- Hedge-crossing and Underworld journeys
- Divination and psychic senses
- Rebellious energy to resist oppression

Connecting to Dandelion

For this meditation we are honoring the energy and essence of dandelion and the spirit of this plant ally. Follow the same steps from the Bindweed meditation.

Seek the spirit of dandelion. Visualize the plant in your mind's eye, call its name, focus your intention on finding the spirit.

Hear or speak the words:

> We call out across the spiritual ecosystem, seeking the All spirit, the great spirit, of dandelion. That nexus spirit which connects all like plants together, sharing their memories, experiences, and wisdom. The witch of the Underworld, dandelion.
> We wish to connect to this magic.
> We call out, in song, to them:
> Come, come, come, dandelion,
> That carries over air

Come, plant spirit that connects spirits,
Come, come forth

Come, come, come, dandelion,
That carries over air
Come, plant spirit that heals,
Come, come forth

Come, come, come, dandelion,
That carries over air
Come, plant spirit that divines,
Come, come forth

Visualization

As you open your Other eyes, find yourself on the edge of an ancient woodland, where the trees are crooked and gnarled by time, their leaves thick and lush.

The sun beams down and creates shafts of light that spotlight the grassy earth below, a tangle of plants and moss, fallen branches, and the flitting of animals into their burrows.

And all about the entrance way are dandelions.

These are dandelions free from impediment, untouched by chemicals or the sanitizing hands of those who would still their growth. Larger than usual, their deep green leaves unfurl with welcome.

They are in different stages, some with their bright yellow faces turning toward the sun, some ready to dance upon the breeze with a wishful puff of air. You can almost hear them singing together on the wind—cheerful, upbeat, and sharing information so freely. Those disembodied voices reminding you of spirits from the Other side—and then you know.

This is an entrance way to the Otherworld.

The trees concave together forming a gateway, the grass and moss a path. On the other side is the realm of the dead, but for now, that is not your destination.

You might hear the whispers from loved ones or guides, but your purpose is to connect with the dandelion spirits who reside here on the edges. The fringe-bound liminal plants who act as psychopomps, bringing forth all other spirits.

You breathe in, and out.

You breathe in, and out.

You breathe in, and out.

You sit comfortably on the grass near the dandelions, opening up your psychic senses in their direction, visualizing your third eye opening and glowing with golden light.

You can feel them turning to you in welcome and interest.

You ground into the space, feeling the earth beneath you as anchor and the air all around tugging at your hair. It is refreshing, clearing away any psychic cobwebs from your mind, bringing clarity and awareness. Your senses feel a little sharper. Colors seem brighter, and the light dances in a way you previously had not noticed.

Your consciousness expands, and you feel how you are more than just your body. More than just your senses. You are spirit, and so too are they.

Dandelion spirit speaks:
Welcome back, Little Ones,
With heavy feet and burdened hearts.
It has been so difficult for a while, has it not?
We know.
We see.
We hear the voices on the wind and see all the connections.
We bring back laughter, being made of it, and wishes.
If you dare to dream, then make a wish, here and now,
And we will see it granted.
Magic is everywhere, and not half the world recalls it.
Seeing only in gray poison lead-lined boxes, so limiting,
All the world a limitation without a joke or a smile,
So fixated on all the wrong things.
We bring back spirit communication and healing,
All the world a stage for plant work,
Come back time and again, do not be a stranger!
For you are most welcome here.

Sit with these words for a while. See how they make you feel.

When you are ready, give thanks to the spirit of the dandelion. You may wish to give an offering of blood or breath (in the spirit world). You can sing or speak words of gratitude. You may wish to drink a libation, such as dandelion tea! See how it makes you feel after doing so and journal that experience too.

Then bow (out of respect), and come back the way you came, along the path, and out of the fields. With each step, reconnect back to the earth, grounding off the excess energy. rounding back into our world.

Open your eyes and come back to yourself.

Your experiences may vary—all are valid! Dandelion will appear howsoever it chooses to each individual in meditation. Listen for further advice. You may wish to ask questions or for their insight when working with the energies of dandelion when you are seeking connection to all spirits of the world, for necromantic rituals, for wishing, and returning to a state of joy.

Spirits of Plants and the Hedgerow

These are some of my personal favorite plant spirits to connect with when seeking to expand your understanding as a hedge witch. The wonderful thing about all these plants is that they have an energy that reminds me of witches. They are often dismissed, ignored, or treated as less than they are, when in fact each of these particular plants has incredible medicinal properties, are edible (although use caution when eating anything you're unsure of) and full of knowledge.

You might want to visualize yourself inviting each of the spirits into a particular section of your inner sacred grove as you build up a rapport with them. Building a relationship with plants can be done in the wild or cultivated in your back garden or in plant pots. You can carry the dried plant with you too and include it in spellwork.

You can use all of these plants in magical ways, of course, for protection and guidance when you seek to walk the spirit worlds. Bindweed vine can be dried and tied around your wrist or ankle to create a "psychic anchor" that can be used when spirit walking. You visualize the bindweed spirit infusing its energy into that bracelet, as a red or gold thread, which you can see around your wrist/ankle in your spirit form (in meditation/

visualization). That thread, when pulled, will bring you right back into your body should you wish to return quickly.

Dandelions make wonderful additions to incenses that help stimulate your psychic senses and assist with crossing the hedge. Dandelion is used to conjure spirits.

Dandelion and nettle tea is widely available and can be drunk ahead of ritual to help you stimulate your psychic senses as well as protect you from harm (from the inside out!). You can wear any (or all) of these plants as a protective charm when engaging in journey work, and of course, request that the spirit of a plant guide you through the Otherworld.

SHADOW SPIRITS OF THE HEDGEROW

The land, and the spirits of the land, carry anger within them. How can they not? Humans have done more harm to this planet in the last hundred years than for the rest of our existence, and corporations continue to kill the environment, the ecosystems, unabashed and without remorse—for profit.

As witches, we cannot ignore that this is happening nor that the spiritual ecosystem would reflect the opinions of nonhuman spirits. I once encountered an angry yew tree in a local woods and worked hard to quell some of his rage. He had been ravaged, harmed, mutilated by teenagers who sprayed him with paint and ripped out his branches.

Humans who think there are no consequences for their actions and are deep in a sense of apathetic entitlement are a plague on this world.

I cried for him, that yew tree.

I also felt a sense of being at a complete loss as to what to do to help the world at large—the environment. It felt like an impossible task, when the powers that be point the fingers at the public using straws and carry on pumping their pollution headlong into the oceans.

All is not lost, though. Groups are making strides, political lobbyists fight governments. Awareness through education is possible, and every little thing you do to try to help in any way is known to the spirits. It is remembered.

Rituals and spells to protect local wildlife and forest areas are also helpful. The worlds are all energy vibrating—not as separate as we might have originally been led to believe. Every use of your energy, every charm, ritual, and spell, can feed the universe, and while, yes, some of your spells will be for worldly concerns (and there is no shame in needing to pay your bills or find love), some can be to give back to the world. Hedge witches walk the worlds for knowledge, to commune with spirits, and when they can, they offer protection and sustenance for them too.

I have mentioned earlier that spirits such as plants and trees will have shadows, because fear and anger are universal emotions within the spiritual ecosystem. The sovereign spirit of each plant and tree absorbs the lessons of all of its kind, and some of those lessons will be negative. Some of the memories will be haunting, frightening, and violent.

When we connect to certain plants and trees, we will also find our own shadows mirrored back at us when the sovereign spirit contains that shadow, similar to how being "poked" by other people's shadows happens.

HEALING YOURSELF, HEALING THE SPIRITS

When you undertake such journeys with the spirits of the hedge, you come to realize that you are simultaneously learning more about yourself and your shadow as well as the shadow that is within that spirit. Thus the first step of healing that shadow is acknowledgement of it—and the acknowledgement that spirits other than humans are just (if not more so) complex, as both a part of us and separate from us.

It is easy to dismiss plants and trees as less alive, less sentient, less intelligent, because their expression is alien to us, and most of humans do ignore the spirits of this world, never mind thinking about healing them. Many people want to save the trees because, frankly, humans will be dead without them, which is fair enough, but to the hedge witch that is only half the story.

This journey of realization is part of societal shadow, maybe even a collective species shadow—the need to believe we are the top of the food chain, smarter than anything else on the planet and in complete control at all times, while we destroy that planet. If anything sounds like the consequence of an unhealed broken shadow psyche, how humans by and large treat nature is one.

We can give our time, effort, money, life force to the preservation of nature in the way that calls us to most as witches. All those amount to the same thing anyway, really—energy. We put our energy into healing ourselves, being gentle with ourselves, learning to love ourselves, and so too those spirits present within our inner sacred grove that we carry with us.

As we do so, our inner world begins to reflect into our manifested reality—we start actively engaging and finding ways of giving energy to the world to help heal it. It is awareness of being part of a physical and spiritual ecosystem—knowing that our thoughts, energy, and actions reverberate and are felt by spirits that exist within that spiritual ecosystem.

It is the knowledge that everything we do has impact.

ANCESTRAL SPIRITS OF HUMANKIND

Most of the spirits we have called to guard and guide us have been nonhuman, for a few reasons. It helps to step outside the standard idea of having a human help you in life, and gets you used to sensing what a nonhuman spirit might look and feel like psychically—so you can tell if a spirit is not human.

This will be of benefit when partaking in spirit world journeys, in case spirits show up as humanoid but your intuition knows that something is awry. Not everything in the spirit worlds is what it appears (or pretends) to be.

We do all have ancestral spirits, though, in the spiritual ecosystem to whom we can connect if we wish. Another reason for waiting this long to discuss human ancestral spirits is the "DNA problem" that causes so many arguments and gatekeeping, even in the European-based witchcraft paths.

Most Europeans will have bloodline connections to one or more of the Celtic peoples in history, because those peoples traveled, traded, and married. Their legacy, therefore, is us. But I am not going to tell someone with limited or no European ancestry that they're less connected to this path. Your ancestors do not have to be tied to this heritage to guard or guide you. They just have to love you and show acceptance.

Something I wish there was more of in the world in general.

Bloodline often shows up in meditation as red threads, and indeed in modern spiritual circles this is frequently used to represent our connection to our ancestral spirits. Those red threads that connect us, invisible stitches woven together by fate, the spider web that shivers in knowing as one like-minded soul reaches out across the spiritual ecosystem to another.

The bloodline of life force in its Otherness, not quite tangible and yet felt so deeply in the chambers of our hearts. The steady beating drum of our ancestors—of blood and spirit—thumping through our veins and bursting unbidden from the recesses of our psyches . . . dreams made manifest, memories singing from the depths, calling . . . calling us home.

The stirring of knowing you are connected to others, honoring it, even when it stings, and the looping back around in the weft of the textile, etching into rivers of blood, and time, and life . . . knowing that fate doesn't care about your excuses, it bids you come, peek behind the veil, know yourself, right yourself, cry and scream and honor all of life—the beauty and the hideousness all swirled in together—it's all the same paint, after all.

The following is a visualization to connect to ancestral spirits.

Visualization: Ancestral Spirits

Close your eyes and breathe deeply. Relax. Let the mundane world fade away. Use meditative music if that helps. Shift your energy inward, seek the tendril of soul that connects you to the spiritual ecosystem.

Begin by allowing your consciousness to drop into heart space—within yourself. Visualize a red thread energy at both your root center and your heart center, glowing red (base) and gold (heart), meeting together like a strand of DNA, and traveling down through your body into the earth.

Connect with the spiritual ecosystem at your base, in what some call the root chakra or the (spirit) womb cauldron. You can also spread your roots through your feet energy centers.

Allow the energy of the spiritual ecosystem to rise through the earth and mesh together with your thread in mutual exchange or balance.

> You are sitting in an ancient cavern, worn by the elements. The cavern is massive, cathedral like in its proportions, with stalagmites and stalactites framing the landscape.
>
> You sit atop warm sand, and beneath you is a spiral. You are at its center.
>
> In here, you can hear the echoes of the whispers of your ancestors on the wind, feel the earth that contains their footsteps, and within you seek the thread to their support, knowing that everything that has been woven or shall ever be woven flows through you.
>
> Here in this space, you are more alive than perhaps you have ever been.
>
> Here in this space you are closer to death than you have ever been.
>
> The balance is within you, in the warp and the weft.
>
> Mistakes make the pattern interesting and unique. Perfection does not exist, except in the knowing that all is perfect, just as it is.
>
> You hold out your hands and see red threads within them, looping over your fingers, around your wrists, and flowing out from you like rivers that vanish into the nether of eternity. All links flow forth from you and to you.
>
> You are connected.
>
> You are alive.
>
> You are home.

Take some time to try this experience. See what you feel and hear. All experiences are valid.

You can use this visualization for the Grandmothers specifically—they who are often thought of as the secret or wisdom keepers in many spiritual circles, honoring the energy and essence of the Hag. We reclaim this archetype as one of power not diminished by aging. Seek the spirit of hags or grandmothers, or wise ones, or crones. Visualize one in your mind's eye, call its name, focus your intention on finding the spirit.

WORKING WITH HUMAN SPIRITS

You can call on specific ancestor spirits too when working at the hedge, if you feel they are open to communicating with you and guiding you in your spiritual journeys. They see things we cannot, and if you travel with a spirit who has your best interest at heart, you will be protected. If you have something of theirs, a memento, you can hold it when meditating and journeying to strengthen this connection.

For myself, I prefer tree or plant spirits. They understand magic better than any human spirit I have ever interacted with. They are more open to the connections of the spiritual ecosystem. It is personal preference, of course, but tree spirits have never let me down, and they are connected to the center of the universe.

ANIMAL SPIRITS WHEN SHAPESHIFTING

So far, we have connected mostly with spirits in the spiritual ecosystem who are guardians and guides, but we should also discuss those spirits we wish to connect with and transform into.

The shape one will likely take when shapeshifting is a highly personal thing, but I do believe we each have a Land spirit, a Sea spirit, and a Sky spirit to which we are most drawn (although this can evolve or change as we do). The call to certain animals seems to reside within a person's soul and is just a part of their soul knowing. There may be little to no discernible reason for the connection, other than a sense of kindred spirit.

It may also relate to the deity you connect with when seeking to learn about the Other realms, and to that end, I am including one of my main shifting shapes in this section: the crow.

Symbolism of crows is an interesting one indeed. I tend to avoid all the death and fear omen versions, because I think that says more about humans fearing intelligent nonhuman beings than anything else.

Crows feature heavily in Celtic lore, especially with the Morrigan, but also with other gods associated with the Otherworld.

In Lady Charlotte Guest's 1877 translation of the Welsh text *The Mabinogion,* the famous shapeshifter and bard Taliesin (now known as Merlin, which was originally a title) states: "I have fled in the semblance of a crow, scarcely finding rest."[74] Guest claims that in some versions of the tale of Owain, he commands an army of ravens, and this tale is continued in *The Fairy-Faith in Celtic Countries* by W. Y. Evans-Wentz, who claimed it was an army of crows and the hero had a crow that always ensured he was victorious. Bran the Blessed was also known as a crow. He was associated with magic, death, and rebirth. His associations with death and the Underworld were common themes when it came to crows—part of the reason humans feared them. Another reason may have been the demonization of crows by the Church as they were considered magical creatures, and many sorcerers could turn into a crow.

The lessons that have thus far been forthcoming under the goddess Morrigan are immeasurable and therefore cannot be summarized under one animal mask. However, none of the invoked aspects of the shapeshifting goddess have left quite so deep of an imprint as that of the crow. For the sake of clarity, the aspect of the goddess Morrigan most frequently communed with is that of Badb—the translation of which name, from the various historical sources, is generally accepted to be "scald crow" or simply "crow" and one of the earliest mentions of which refers to her as a *bodb catha*, "the battle crow" from the "Wooing of Emer" in the *Dindshenchas*.

It is said that crows are masters of time, that they perceive past, present, and future simultaneously and thus hint at the nonlinear movement of time. This makes them an ideal companion for shapeshifting through the realms!

Humans often refuse to see the world outside of the scope of their own experiences, mired in the limiting belief that their understanding of the world is the only (or best) one. Crow wisdom is immediately unsettling in that it challenges this and any other rigidly held worldview, asking us to sit within the prospect of being utterly wrong. This is not a position that is comfortable to most, conditioned as we are to always seek the right answer and appear correct and therefore powerful.

Perhaps this energy is one of the reasons that crows are frequently reviled and treated with distrust, for even in their physical forms they present themselves with an otherworldly intellect and playful nature, reminding humans that we are not the only creatures with intelligence.

Furthermore, the carrion crow was present and feasting on battlefields, an association that gave rise to their mythological associations with death and gods and goddesses of war such as the Morrigan. The Celts believed that the crows were ferrying the souls of the dead to the Otherworld by consuming the flesh, and it was said that the Morrigan could shapeshift into this form, often to signify her hand in a situation, the most renowned example being of a crow landing on Cú Chulainn (her favored warrior) at his death.

The concept of death certainly brings forth human speculation of the unknown, for as much as we theorize, it remains the ultimate inescapable truth and yet unknowable mystery. It is beyond human control, no matter what methods we employ, and so it should come as no surprise that it falls under the crow mask.

Each time meditation has lent itself to the donning of crow eyes, my human perception must be abandoned. Be it in experiencing the flight of a shapeshifted crow or accessing a different realm in which to visualize yet another aspect of the goddess Morrigan, no two experiences have been the same.

The unpredictability of the crow mask is, by design, unsettling, which is exactly the point—to submerge the individual into the depths of the unknown and the unknowable, inviting them to abandon their limited perceptions. Ultimately, the mask of the crow invites us to simultaneously trust our instincts as well as question everything.

Crow spirits teach us that ultimately we do not (and perhaps, cannot) have a definitive answer, and so we settle on what resonates within us at the time . . . to the question of who we are at that point in time.

In summary, you never know what you're about to see when you shapeshift with crow energy.

VISUALIZATION: CROW SPIRIT

Close your eyes and breathe deeply. Relax. Let the mundane world fade away. Use meditative music if that helps. Shift your energy inward, seek the tendril of soul that connects you to the spiritual ecosystem.

Begin by allowing your consciousness to drop into heart space—within yourself. Visualize a pulsing crow feather at your heart center, glowing with a sheen of blue/purple, and traveling down through your body into the earth. Visualize your feet as crow feet.

Connect with the spiritual ecosystem at your base, in what some call the root chakra or the (spirit) womb cauldron. You can also spread your roots through your feet energy centers.

Allow the energy of the spiritual ecosystem to rise through the earth and mesh together with your thread in mutual exchange or balance.

Seek the spirit of Crow. Visualize one in your mind's eye, call its name, focus your intention on finding the spirit.

Crow is intelligent, curious, full of wonder and hidden knowledge. Frequently Crow shows up in semi-humanoid form, wrapped in a black cloak, covered in archaic black lettering on their limbs. This time, Crow is feminine, but as shapeshifters, they will change in a blink of an eye.

Speaking of eyes, Crow has deep brown eyes, almost black, that shimmer with the energy of the stars, connecting you to the deep universal mysteries by staring into them. Today she wears a black mask over her eyes and nose, hooked with a beak, and decorated with feathers. She unlaces the ribbons from behind her hood, and lets it fall, shaking out long black waves of hair, and grins, beckoning you with clawed fingers.

Crow speaks:

> I foresaw your coming, of course. Welcome.
>
> Welcome to the ancient roads, between worlds, where mysteries hum and secrets blossom. We could go hunting all the ancient tomes I've been writing if you like—I keep misplacing them. They have a kind of life of their own, stories. You start one and suddenly it has run away with you. Strange, isn't it?
>
> I like the wyrd and wonderful places, which are everywhere if you know how to look. Shall I teach you to see them? Will it change you entirely if I did? One can never tell how a single drop of insight might ripple outward.

Your experiences may vary—all are valid! Crow is a shapeshifter and will change depending on who is speaking to them or what message they wish to convey. You may wish to ask questions or for their insight when working with the energies of Crow, when you are seeking answers from the universe, empowering your magical self, seeking to go on a journey or hear messages from the spirit world, or engaged in death work.

SPIRIT RELATIONSHIPS IN THE PHYSICAL WORLD: SACRED SPACE AND SPIRIT PROTECTION

In the space in which I perform most of my witchcraft, I have chosen to create points of power in each of the corners relating to the standard four elements, Earth, Air, Fire, and Water, making sure that there is artwork on the walls representing all the spirits I work with regularly. Even though Fire is not part of the three Celtic realms (as it is created and extinguished) I feel the need to honor it.

In the Earth corner, there is a mini altar space dedicated to the guardian spirits to whom I connect through the spiritual ecosystem, including the examples I have already given for you to connect with. A constant place of reverence, a home and a place to honor the spirits who guide and guard my spirit as I walk through the spiritual ecosystem, seems both necessary and polite. If you were never given a seat at the table but were always expected to attend the meeting, you would be annoyed, right?

Spirit housing is a popular topic among many forms of spirit practice in witchcraft, with many witches, myself included, using bones as spirit housing for different spirits. This using of a bone to create spirit housing is most frequently used for human or animal spirits, with little attention paid to the fact that you do have bones, skin, and hair for trees—it just doesn't have quite the same gothic aesthetic. You can gather bark, berries, and leaves from a tree who has willingly shed them for you and create a kind of spirit housing for it, either in its rough form or, as I prefer, by creating a creature form for the spirit.

You can weave the components of your tree or plant into a poppet or doll, in any form you feel called to (and it is worth communing with the spirit in meditation beforehand to ask if they have any preferences). This becomes the spirit vessel or spirit housing that your spirit can enjoy in the physical world. It creates a physical link (tether) to you as a practicing hedge witch, and gives you something to hold and carry with you when engaging in journey work. It further connects you and the spirit and your relationship.

If you cultivate a relationship with a particular spirit when it comes to walking between worlds, you might utilize the wood as a physical prop to either create protection or to open the doors between worlds. Many witches use staves, stangs, or wands in their hedge-crossing practice. A stang is thought by witches to be possessed by the witch god to assist them in opening themselves up to such journeys.

Witches may use wands or staves to create protective circles spiritually around themselves (and call in the spirits, as we discussed earlier with the tree spirits). Hedge witches may also utilize a wooden athame (ritual knife) or wand to cut through the fabric of reality in their spiritual rites. I prefer the use of my wooden branch of ivy as a "key." I visualize locking and unlocking myself from my body to shapeshift when already in sacred space.

You might also surround yourself with aspects of your spirit in the circle to keep yourself protected, such as a circle of rowan berries, or bark in the four quarters, for example, while calling on the spirit to protect you. A chant for this:

> Spirit of (tree),
> Ancient guardian and spirit friend,
> I ask that you guard my body
> And guide my spirit
> As I travel the realms.

You might also wish to honor and ask for the protection of the spirits of the three realms of Land, Sky, and Sea. Having the essence of a place on your side is no small thing if you get into trouble when shapeshifting. It will call you home.

SPIRIT PROTECTION FOR SHAPESHIFTING OR TRAVELING THROUGH REALMS

Not all spirits are friendly, and some resent humans. Many are indifferent. Some are vicious. If the spirit world reflects into our world, then the natural world should clue you into this idea: predators exist in every walk of life, and humans are perfectly edible.

In the spirit realm, any damage that occurs to your spirit will occur to you. The body makes what the mind experiences real. We don't feel pain until the mind realizes that we're hurt—its power over us is incredible. That's why we must treat this pivotal exercise into hedge witchery with complete respect and the proper caution.

- Learn as much as you can about the process and what to expect before attempting spirit travel.
- Have an experienced practitioner with you or someone who knows you well enough to recognize signs that you might be in trouble.
- Decide which realm you are visiting beforehand, and affirm this out loud (higher, lower, middle).
- Cleanse your space and have protective wards in place to prevent spirit interference in your home.
- Cast a circle of protection with spirits in the quarters.
- Call in your gods to guide and protect you.
- Call in your personal spirits to guide and guard you.
- Use a physical tether (anchor) such as bindweed and visualize the cord of this glowing red around your wrist/ankle, so that you might return to your body immediately.
- State ahead of time you will only spend so much time shapeshifting, so you don't get lost or enraptured in the process. Have an alarm clock if needed.
- Draw protective symbols (such as the Ogham) on your body and "see" the spirit imprint of these in your spirit form.
- Wear protective charms.

Cleansing and Warding Your Home

Prior to any ritual involving spirits, it is wise to cleanse the space your body is in and create wards. Cleansing a home uses magical tools to clear the energy within. Sound is a powerful way to change the vibration, using a drum or bell or rattle, and you can clear the energy with smoke or water. Burning cedar is a wonderful way to cleanse with a European herb, or you can use mugwort.

One of the best pieces of advice I ever heard for keeping your home safe is to give your house a name. Interact with the spirit of your home. Feed it energy. Interact with it daily. Thank it for all that it does, keeping you safe from the elements and other people.

This to some is the creation of a spirit or thoughtform—an egregore, a spirit creation with a task in mind that is constantly linked to you.

I wonder if houses have spirits anyway, as technically they're human spirit housing, and people come and go and sometimes die in them, leaving the house full of energy and memory. At what point does this become separate from a kind of spiritual symbiosis with humans? I am uncertain. But houses seem to have personalities all their own.

Wards are spiritual protective beacons that pick up on spirit threats and repel them, with most people drawing on the art of magical symbols to do this. It is the same method as earlier, when you tap into an Ogham as a gateway to the sovereign tree behind it, only you tap into a symbol that connects to the protective vibration behind it. You can use Ogham for this purpose too, combining several if you prefer.

Some people like to paint these onto their walls before painting over them, or you can use a protective oil to trace them. You can also use a protective tree branch to trace the energetic signature onto your walls. Visualize the symbol glowing and hear it locking the space like a key in a lock.

A Rowan Protection Charm

1. Add nine rowan berries and nine pieces of rowan bark to a red charm bag.
2. On a piece of paper, write your name, and across it draw the Ogham for rowan (Luis).
3. Ask the spirit of the rowan to consecrate and empower this protection spell:

"Rowan protect this body and spirit of mine,
By berry, bark, and breath of nine."

4. Breathe into the pouch nine times, representing the universal life force of inspiration and magic (Awen in the Welsh tradition).

The Anchor

It is highly recommended to wear or hold a physical anchor when attempting to travel between realms, something that contains a part of your body (such as hair or nails) woven with a protective spirit (such as bindweed, whose tenacity is second to none). Connect yourself energetically to this anchor so it will provide a thread to guide you back from the spirit world if needed. If you have someone with you, set a time and agreed-upon method to bring you back fully to the waking world.

HOW TO SHAPESHIFT AND TRAVEL THROUGH THE OTHER WORLDS

Before we begin shapeshifting, it seems prudent to discuss some of the ways in which the practitioner might seek to reach an alternative energetic state, such as being within trance, which often feels like a mixture of hyperawareness mixed with intoxication.

Each person will experience their own heightened energetic state differently, but the general objective is to feel "other"—when your senses swim, your perception shifts, you feel your mind slip from the confinements of the material world and gain a sense of that which people label as "supernatural." Colors are more vibrant, sounds seem alien, and your inner self seems to revel and surge with excitement. It may feel as you are seeing the world as the mundane and magical reveal how truly merged they are.

This is the gateway of those who walk between worlds, the hedge witch and the shapeshifter. To pass through is to walk with spirits, to hear the echoes and insights of Otherness. Here shall we dwell.

THE ART OF ECSTATIC CONNECTION

There are many methods that may be called traditional and have been relied upon by magical practitioners throughout the collective human history to reach elevated states of consciousness. It is through the practice of some, or indeed all, of these that the individual finds their best personal needs.

The first step is often to declare your intention to move beyond the usual state you occupy and enter into ritual, which is most commonly done by preparing the body and auric field by processes of cleaning and cleansing. This may involve engaging in ritual bathing and then changing one's attire to either specific magical garb or the discarding of clothing altogether. Most practitioners recommend cleaning your body first to remove any physical residue from everyday life, and then cleansing yourself in a ritual manner to align your mind and your energy with the intention you set before yourself.

When connecting to animal spirits, you may wish to use personal discernment as to whether you wish to be fully cleaned or instead carry elements of dirt and sweat with you. Animalistic spirits know the value of such things in a way that human beings either forget or seek to sanitize away. This may also depend on the energy behind the animal spirit in question. Cat energy is far more groomed than pig energy, for example.

You can always try multiple methods of cleaning and cleansing in preparation for the ritual connection and shapeshifting techniques, and document which is more powerful in your estimation of your experiences.

For a general starting point, it is worth noting that most animals have a preference for the natural over the highly synthesized and perfumed, a vibration that is likely to reverberate through the spiritual ecosystem. Natural soaps, cleansers, and bathing materials are therefore advised if ritual bathing is a common practice for your ritual setup. Salt and herbs in combination make a powerful ingredient in which to create a ritual bath, and water is a potent conduit between the realms of spirits. Water is a connective force that all living beings require, and all the dead remember. It is also thought to carry souls across realms in most cultures.

By stepping into the cleansing bath, you declare your intention and set your mind to work altering your conscious state for the first time. You may call upon the spirits of the water and the herbs to aid you or call in your ancestral line or other spirit allies. If you are unsure as to any of these things, simply declare the intention to travel between worlds and learn from the spirits.

Stepping into the bath or cleansing space, begin to focus on the energy of the chosen spirit with whom you wish to connect. You may wish to read ahead to be prepared, and have set up an altar space dedicated to the chosen spirit, which we shall discuss in more depth later. If this is the case, you may choose to carry a bone, droplets of blood, feather, claw, or tooth into the cleansing area and place within the water if you so choose, or on the side of the bath where you can focus on its energies.

It is worth noting that certain animal products can smell when they get wet, especially if they are not fully cleaned of flesh material before. This can be an enlightening albeit acrid and pungent experience and really depends on the nature of the practitioner as to whether such smells and possibly flesh matter will cause them to be unable to continue with the rite.

It is worth considering that death, decay, and all the associated sensory experiences are part of the realm of necromancy, of honoring the death processes and the spirits that lay beyond mortal flesh. Human beings have sought to sanitize away the death processes, and so confronting any feelings of revulsion or apprehension around scents, sights, and experiences is a worthy endeavor.

If you do choose to incorporate part of the animal in your ritual bathing, it is akin to coating your skin in the scent and energy of the animal (even if the scent is less literal and more of a metaphysical exercise). Make sure it is fully sanitized first though, please. The human sense of smell is incredibly limited, but animals are far less inhibited. Through it many of them recognize one another, protect their territory and each other, chose partners and mate, and form complex attachments based largely on scent.

The act of submerging yourself in the conduit of water infused with animal aroma is an act of greeting. To step beyond the confinements of human experience and merge with the spirits denotes a willingness and appreciation for the power and knowledge to be imparted later.

If you cannot access an animal part, for whatever reason, you may wish to add an energetic understudy to the bathing ritual, something that speaks to you of the spirit in question. This is deeply personal and based on your own intuition, but it could be herbs or leaves from their natural habitat, or something they might feed on. You can bring the essence of their environment into your space—which is much like the connectedness of stepping into nature where the animal lives but in reverse, bringing it to you instead.

If you visit their environment first to collect the leaves, then this becomes a mini ritual of symbiosis in itself—you journey to the physical environment of the animal, and then bring that essence into your home (and yourself). You feel the same ground beneath your feet, listen to their call, sense the energy of the animal in nature, perhaps leaving a part of yourself behind to connect you to the space with a few drops of your own blood and life essence.

As you return, you take a wild harvest with you, to deepen that connection, and take it into water to shift the energies into the realm of spirits. You draw the essence of the animal through the water, to be surrounded and submerged within it, taking that energy within. You may wish to listen to music that incorporates the sounds you associate with the animal, whether it be their direct call or cry or a looser interpretation, perhaps sounds of their environment.

This space is the beginning of a sensory overload that attaches you to the energetic match of the spirit you seek. To be fully submerged within their consciousness is to take a part of them into your own being, to shift into their energy.

Below, this concept is put into a practical mini ritual format, which can be practiced separately as well as part of the overall deeper connective rituals to each individual animal spirit.

The greater art of shapeshifting is not to seek to simply change one's shape, connect with one spirit, or understand the lesson of one animal, spirit, or being, but instead to connect to the whole physical and spiritual ecosystem. It is a form of shapeshifting that draws on the animistic beliefs and informs us of spiritual information the same way our body interacts with an environment. At any given point the body is a multifunctioning hub, as the many parts of the self accrue information from various forms of stimuli, acting both independently and in conjunction. Our senses all work as part of the whole, feeding information to our personal nexus—the mind, the brain—which filters through the hundreds of thousands of moments of energetic interplay and decides on what level of response is merited, if the information is barely stored or if an emotional or physical reaction is required.

Danger or the perception of it within an environment, for example, warrants the immediate fight-or-flight response. Most of the information, though, is subconsciously processed and we barely even notice it, if we do at all. Breath is not considered unless we draw purposeful attention to it. In this manner, our body is drawing in energy signals from the location within which we find ourselves, as we push our energy out into that space to gather that information, some of it from our conscious minds with a sense of deliberateness, some of it from routine and habit and the subconscious.

We shapeshift our consciousness outward into the whole ecosystem every time we seek to interact with it. Becoming hyperaware and unconsciously collecting information all at once, we connect to all parts of the environment. In this sense, the greater art of shapeshifting is also that of living alchemy; at every given moment we are shapeshifting in processes that we do not usually consider, in a state of permanent personal transmutation. Our bodies grow, go through cycles, cells perform functions and die off, our skin sheds, we breathe in oxygen and remove toxins, all without much energy being expended on considering why the body performs such functions. Instead, we trust that inner shapeshift as natural and necessary.

We transmute the world around us—seen and unseen—constantly through the process of living alchemy through the vessel of our own mind and body and deepen our connection to it. At times we do seek to become aware of some of the shapeshifting processes.

A Wilder Home

The following ritual is designed to form an energetic connection between the practitioner and the habitat of a particular animal, strengthening the bond and understanding, which will later add to the power of the communication with spirits and the magic performed in conjunction with them.

It has the added benefit of creating a connection with the *genius loci*, the protective spirit of the land in which you are performing magic, and as all things are connected in the realm of spirit, appeasing the land spirits can only be of future benefit.

The journeying to a particular area to engage in spirit work can be seen as a sort of pilgrimage, through which the practitioner takes on the archetype of the traveler.

- Location: A place within nature that is home to the animal whose spirit you wish to form a deeper understanding of.
- Required materials: Foraging tools and a container (bag) to carry back material items, a lancet to draw blood, water.

The traveler is an archetype of movement, who treats each land into which they venture as an experience, seeking to capture profound moments as memories, creating new neural pathways by submerging themselves into each element of this foreign environment, taking in the unusual sights, scents, and sounds. Through the embodiment of the traveler, the hedge witch begins to appreciate the parallels of this pathwalking to the eventual connection with the animalistic spirit beyond the masks.

To walk as the incarnations of that spirit walk, to touch the same ground, breathe the same air, taste the same scents on the wind, to know how the spirit experiences its preferred habitat, is to begin to know the spirit itself.

When embodying the traveler, a magical practitioner learns to practice the art of the waking meditative state, to both relax the conscious mind so that it might shift into the vibration of spiritual awareness while still observing their surroundings.

Plan ahead when visiting areas, make sure you know viable routes to travel. When you arrive, spend some time meditating if you are safe to do so in this spot, and connect to the spirit with whom you wish to shift your shape into the likeness of. You will want to forage some of the natural environment to take back with you for your venture into shapeshifting, and leave behind some of your life force. I do this by leaving a drop of blood, but you could leave breath or spit if you have no sanitary way of drawing blood. You could also leave appropriate food for them.

Thank all the spirits who have attended you in this. Bring back dirt, feathers, whatever you could find. If unsuccessful, try repeat attempts and build up your relationship with the spirit.

Home from Home

When you have returned to your space, you might try a secondary small ritual, to permeate every inch of yourself with connection the animal in question. If you bought back a little dirt or water from its environment, place this in a bowl in your home and visualize its energy reaching out, covering everything. Feel the connection take place between habitats. See your space become a mirror for the one out in nature. Tie those energetic threads together in your mind's eye.

Meditate in the space until you feel as though you're back outside, with all the same sights, smells, and sounds. Welcome the spirit of the animal here with you, not only separate from you but a part of you. Unlock it within your own soul space. See it within your own inner sacred grove. Know that it is a part of you.

You can become it.

OTHER FORMS OF SPIRITUAL ECSTASY

There are other methods that a hedge witch might tap into to change their vibrational state. I have not included any recipes for witch ointments, which usually consist of psychotropic plant materials that can, in the wrong hands, be dangerous. If you do not know what you're doing when it comes to poisonous baneful plants and you still want to use a witch ointment, seek out a licensed professional. The ointments are usually placed on the wrists and ankles and have a sedative effect that eases the mind and body and opens the psychic senses.

Dance and drumming and music are the most common techniques used to help a hedge witch change their energetic vibration. Your mood, your energy, the state that you're in are all powerfully affected by sound and movement. Deep rhythmic breathing, a concentration on breath work and dropping into your body, and moving that body in deliberate action that builds from slow movement to frenzy, are all ways of entering trance.

Entering a trance state before you travel is to assist yourself in stepping outside your body. It gives your active mind the signal to stop engaging with the mundane world and let the magical self take over. Relax your body, alter your state of consciousness . . . that is the way to open the door. You may also benefit from burning a hedge-crossing incense, which you can purchase if you prefer or you can craft your own. Try this general hedge-crossing incense blend:

Dandelion root: 3 tsp
Dittany of Crete: 1 tsp
Mugwort: 1 tsp
Mullein: 1 tsp
Myrrh: 1 tsp
Poppy seed: 1 small pinch
Rowan berries: 3 berries

General Shapeshifting Guide for the Experience Itself

- Cleanse and protect your home, including warding and creating protective amulets.
- Set out any tools you are using (poppet for spirit companion, charms, object to assist you traveling, your spirit mask).
- Decide which form you are to take, and which realm you wish to travel to and for what purpose, which spirits you would like to see (create an intention for your spirit travel).
- Create safe boundaries around yourself, including a friend if you are doing so, sacred space, and timing limits.
- Invoke in spirits to protect and guide you.
- Check all of your protections beforehand—spirit tethers, amulets, sigils on your skin.
- Engage in ecstatic connection to alter your consciousness.
- Lie down or sit to go inward and begin your visualization.

Key Points to Remember Before Shapeshifting

- Have a clear and defined purpose and a time limit. It is tempting to keep going when spirit traveling, but you can risk fatigue, spirit loss, injury, and spirit attachment if you push yourself too far too soon.
- Listen to your guides and guards at all times.
- If you feel even slightly at risk, pull the spirit cord and come back to yourself.
- Be polite and honorable to any spirits you meet, but do not make promises or deals at this stage.
- Do not give away your life force in the spirit world.
- Do not take off your protections.
- Do not assume any spirit is who they claim to be—after all, you're not really the spirit whose form you took.
- The first few times you shapeshift, you may want to stay close to the world tree and come back relatively quickly until you're well versed in the practice and how it feels.

THE SHAPESHIFTING RITUAL VISUALIZATION

A journey to take after all preparations have been met.

Close your eyes.

Focus on your breathing, and with each breath let it fill you more deeply, and pull your consciousness downward.

Let the first breath fill your head, the second your lungs, and pull the third breath deep into your stomach.

Breathe deeper, and deeper, letting your consciousness go inward.

Shift your energy inward, seek the tendril of soul that connects you to the spiritual ecosystem.

> Begin by allowing your consciousness to drop into heart space—within yourself. Visualize a beating drum energy that almost howls from within at your heart center, glowing deep red, and with each pulse traveling downward, down through your body into the earth.
>
> Connect with the spiritual ecosystem at your base, in what some call the root chakra, or the (spirit) womb cauldron. You can also spread your roots through your feet energy centers.
>
> Allow the energy of the spiritual ecosystem to rise through the earth and mesh together with your thread in mutual exchange or balance.
>
> Instead of allowing your energy to flow outward into the ecosystem, return inward. Enter through the cauldron you have chosen for the appropriate realm, go inside the dark pool at its center, and follow the thread down into your inner sacred grove. It is dark within to start with, and you are alone in the darkness of yourself. You can hear the trees rustling and the wind between their branches.
>
> Within your inner sacred grove you are seeking the axis mundi, the world tree, the center point between all realms, inner and outer.
>
> There is no mistaking the axis mundi—it thrums with power, it is of spirit and bark, otherworldly and central, the keeper of all keys, the crossroads to all realms.
>
> You walk toward it, knowing that you will travel to another realm. You will shift your shape as you engage with this tree, this mighty spirit.

At the base of the world tree, you see your mask waiting for you. The mask that when you place it on your face will begin the transformation, for written into its very fabric is the essence of the animal you shall become.

You reach down, and admire it. This tool of the hedge witch—this creation of yours. That which will allow you to shift and change. Step outside of your skin.

Place the mask upon your face, and feel the fabric of the universe pressing into you, calling you to be more than you are, to travel, to learn. To know what it means to be a hedge witch.

You feel at once the awkwardness of your current shape, the lumbering inelegant nature of the human form, and want to shirk free of it. You can feel your skin crawling, and you twist with every ache as your bones seem to creak and your body folds in on itself.

You fold in and in and in again, a process of becoming and unbecoming, giving life to the spirit that resides within your spirit, allowing it to come forth.

Seeing through animalistic eyes of Otherness.

You become.

You revel in your new form, free, lighter, more agile and swift, more adapted to traveling your chosen realm. You make your way into the center of the world tree and travel along it in your chosen direction—making your way to that realm.

You intuitively know when you have reached it, as the energy around you seems to shift, beckoning you to this realm, full of wonder. This realm where the spirits roam freely, and everything is more of itself, closer to its soul identity, the colors more vibrant, the sounds more crisp, as if the dull scales of the mortal world have fallen away.

Your time here is limited, and you glimpse the thread around you, a reminder to be careful, and listen to your guides. You look around, and call out for them. Hearing you, they step out from the world tree too, beckoned by your connection, your respect for them, and your need. You check to see your spirit amulet is still in place.

When satisfied, you follow your spirit, seeking out those who will speak to you. Of magic, of the world, of prophecy, of fate. You seek wonders.

> When the timer ticks down, it is time to return, and return you must, as your guardian tells you.
>
> Turn from this place; you may return, it is not a once in a lifetime trip. Even if you feel sad to leave, you must return back the way you came, to the world tree. Follow the tree back to yourself, back to your body, back to the waking world.
>
> Reenter your human form, stretching at every edge of your shape-shifted self, growing larger, stretching out and out and out . . . Feel yourself rising back up through your consciousness, up through the sky of the inner sacred grove, up, up, up and out through the Cauldron of Warming at your base, into your body, up through the heart space of the Cauldron of Motion, up to the Cauldron of Wisdom in your head.

Come back to your waking body. Open your eyes, wiggle your hands, feet, and all of your body to shake off the meditative state.

Future Journeys

It is worth noting that it takes practice to lift yourself out of yourself in meditation and to travel between worlds. You may need several attempts to even get there in the first place. I recommend starting with the lower world, being most connected to witches and magic.

Space out your trips of shapeshifting, as you do not want to become addicted in a form of escapism out of the body nor risk harm to yourself.

CONCLUSION

The journey of the Celtic hedge witch is one of wonder. I hope within these pages, something like inspiration has found you.

> May the land ground you,
> The sky inspire you,
> And sea restore you.
> As it is in the Otherworld,
> So it is in this world.
> Travel well.

NOTES

1. Emma Restall Orr, *The Wakeful World: Animism, Mind, and the Self in Nature* (Moon Books, 2012), 107.
2. Lloyd Graham, "Echoes of Antiquity in the Early Irish 'Song of Amergin,'" academia.edu.
3. Plato, *The Republic of Plato, The Ten Books, Complete and Unabridged* (Penguin Classics of Greek Philosophy, 2021), 70.
4. Plato, *Phaedrus* (Penguin Classics, 2005), 361.
5. Cambridge dictionary online, dictionary.cambridge.org.
6. Merriam-Webster Dictionary online, www.merriam-webster.com.
7. Three Initiates, *The Kybalion, Hermetic Philosophy* (St. Martin's Essentials, 2020), 14.
8. Katherine Hurst, "7 Hermetic Principles: Laws of the Universe According to the Kybalion," thelawofattraction.com.
9. Ibid.
10. Lucien Lévy-Bruhl, *L'Experience Mystique et Les Symboles Chez les Primitifs*. (Librarie Felix Alcan, 1938), 183.
11. Cambridge Dictionary online, dictionary.cambridge.org.

12. National Trust, Wallington, nationaltrust.org.uk.
13. People's Trust for Endangered Species, Hedgerow Wildlife, ptes.org.
14. Etymology online, etymonline.com.
15. The British Druid Order, www.druidry.co.uk.
16. Rae Beth, *The Green Hedge Witch* (Crowood Press, 2018).
17. Oxford Reference online, oxfordreference.com.
18. Collins dictionary online, collinsdictionary.com.
19. Della Hooke, *Trees in Anglo-Saxon England* (Boydell, 2010), 96
20. Lebor na hUidre, trans. Eugene O'Curry, "The Sick-bed of Cuchulain, and the Only Jealousy of Emer" ("Serglige Con Culainn ocus Óenét Emire").
21. Oxford English Dictionary online, oed.com.
22. Joseph Falaky Nagy, "Orality in Medieval Irish Narrative: An Overview," Oral Tradition 1/2 (1986): 272–301.
23. Sharon Paice MacLeod, *Celtic Cosmology and the Otherworld* (McFarland, 2018), 11.
24. Leon O'Cathasaigh, "Tír Na nÓg: The Legend of Oisín, Niamh and the Land of Eternal Youth," Irish Central, irishcentral.com.
25. *The Mabinogion,* trans. Sioned Davies, Oxford World's Classics (Oxford University Press, 2007), 41
26. Danu Forest, *Wild Magic: Celtic Folk Traditions for the Solitary Practitioner* (Llewellyn, 2020), 13
27. John Carey, "The Location of the Otherworld in Irish Tradition," *Éigse 19* (1982): 36–43.
28. Liam Mac Mathúna, "Irish Perceptions of the Cosmos," *Celtica* 23 (1999): 174–175.
29. Cecile O'Rahilly, trans. and ed., *Táin Bó Cúalnge from the Book of Leinster* (Dublin Institute for Advanced Studies, 1967).

30. *The Mabinogion,* Lady Charlotte Guest, trans., 1877, sacred-texts.com.

31. Erynn Rowan Laurie, trans., "The Cauldron of Poesy," *Obsidian,* obsidianmagazine.com.

32. Ibid.

33. Nathaniel Hughes and Fiona Owen, *Intuitive Herbalism* (Quintessence, 2019).

34. Online Etymology Dictionary, etymonline.com.

35. Bob Curran, *Complete Guide to Celtic Mythology* (Appletree, 2000).

36. Erynn Rowan Laurie, trans., *The Cauldron of Poesy,* in *The Druid's Primer,* Luke Eastwood (Moon Books, 2012), 283.

37. CELT: The Corpus of Electronic Texts, "The Irish Version of the Historia Britonum of Nennius," celt.ucc.ie.

38. John Shaw, "A Gaelic Eschatological Folktale, Celtic Cosmology, and Dumézil's 'Three Realms,'" *Journal of Indo-European Studies* 35 (2007): 250. Also in Jacqueline Borsje et al., eds., *Celtic Cosmology: Perspectives from Ireland and Scotland* (Pontifical Institute of Mediaeval Studies, 2014).

39. Lucius Annaeus Sencca, *Moral Epistles,* Richard M. Gummere, trans., Loeb Classical Library, vol. I (Harvard University Press, 1917).

40. Ronald Hutton, *Blood and Mistletoe: The History of the Druids in Britain* (Yale University Press, 2009), 11

41. Order of Bards, Ovates and Druids, druidry.org.

42. Grigory Bondarenko, *Studies in Irish Mythology* (Curach Bhán Publications, 2014), academia.edu.

43. Della Hooke, *Trees in Anglo-Saxon England* (Boydell, 2010), 96

44. Elizabeth A. Gray, ed. and trans., *Cath Maige Tuired: The Second Battle of Mag Tuired* (Irish Texts Society, 1982).

45. Sharon Blackie, "Marrying the Land: How We Broke the Ancient Bargain," sharonblackie.substack.com.

46. Sandra Billington and Miranda Green, eds., *The Concept of the Goddess* (Routledge, 1996).

47. Elizabeth A. Gray, ed. and trans., *Cath Maige Tuired: The Second Battle of Mag Tuired* (Irish Texts Society, 1982).

48. Emerald Isle, "Oweynagat," emeraldisle.ie.

49. A. H. Leahy, trans. and ed., "Cattle-Raid of Regamna," in *Romances of Ireland*, vol. I (David Nutt, 1906).

50. Sharon Paice MacLeod, *Celtic Cosmology and the Otherworld* (McFarland, 2018), 116.

51. Kuno Meyer, trans., "The Wooing of Emer," *Archaeological Review* 1 (1888), via Rosalind Clark, "Aspects of the Morrígan in Early Irish Literature," *Irish University Review* 17, no. 2 (Autumn 1987).

52. David Rankine and Sorita D'Este, *The Guises of the Morrigan* (Avalonia, 2005), 26.

53. "The Metrical Dindshenchas," author unknown, celt.ucc.ie.

54. A. H. Leahy, trans. and ed., "The Cattle-Raid of Regamna," excerpted from *Romances of Ireland*, vol. II (David Nutt, 1906), maryjones.us.

55. Online Etymology Dictionary, etymonline.com.

56. Kim Taplin, *Tongues in Trees: Studies in Literature and Ecology* (Green Books, 1989).

57. rneighbors.org.

58. *The Hanes Taliesin,* from the thirteenth-century *Red Book of Hergest,* cited in Robert Graves, *The White Goddess,* 1948.

59. Ian Firla, "The Narrative Structures of Robert Graves' Historical Fiction: A Progression Toward a Conception of the Hero in History," thesis for the University of Leicester, 1998.

60. Mark A. Carter, *Stalking the Goddess* (Moon Books, 2012).

61. Gertrude Clarke Nuttall, *Trees and How They Grow* (Cassell, 1913).

62. "The Wife of Usher's Well," available at bartleby.com.

63. Ivo Dominguez, *Of Spirits: The Book of Rowan* (Sapfire, 2001).

64. John Arnott MacCulloch, *Celtic Mythology* (Dover, 2004).

65. "The Death of Cú Chulainn," *Book of Leinster,* maryjones.us.

66. William Sayers, "Conall's Welcome to Cet in the Old Irish Scéla Mucce Meic Dathó," *Florilegium* 4 (1982): 100–108.

67. "The Hostel of the Quicken Trees," shee-eire.com.

68. *Táin Bó Cúailnge* (TBC II) 2528–2529, maryjones.us.

69. In 1597, King James VI of Scotland published a compendium on witchcraft lore called *Daemonologie*.

70. John Bell, ed., *Rhymes of Northern Bards, 1812,* "The Laidley Worm of Spindleston-Heugh," written by Duncan Frasier in 1270.

71. Sir James George Frazer, *The Golden Bough* (1922).

72. The Lanunga, tenth-century Anglo-Saxon charm (one of nine).

73. Rebecca Beyer, "A Tale of Spring: The Lion's Tooth," bloodandspicebush.com.

74. *The Mabinogion,* Lady Charlotte Guest, trans., 1877, sacred-texts.com.

BIBLIOGRAPHY

Beth, Rae. *The Green Hedge Witch,* 2nd ed. Crowood Press, 2018.
Beth, Rae. *The Hedge Witch's Way: Magical Spirituality for the Lone Spellcaster.* Crowood Press, 2006.
Blackie, Sharon. *If Women Rose Rooted.* September Publishing, 2016.
Billington, Sandra, and Miranda Green, eds. *The Concept of the Goddess.* Routledge, 1996.
Boyer, Connie. *Under the Bramble Arch.* Troy Books, 2020.
Carey, John. "The Location of the Otherworld in Irish Tradition," *Éigse* 19 (1982): 36–43.
Curran, Bob. *Complete Guide to Celtic Mythology.* Appletree, 2000.
Davies, Sioned, trans. *The Mabinogion.* Oxford University Press, 2007.
Dominguez Jr., Ivo. *Of Spirits: The Book of Rowan.* Sapfire Productions, 2001.
Forest, Danu. *Wild Magic: Celtic Folk Traditions for the Solitary Practitioner.* Llewellyn Publications, 2020.
Elizabeth A. Gray, ed. and trans. *Cath Maige Tuired: The Second Battle of Mag Tuired.* Irish Texts Society, 1982.
Grimassi, Raven. *Grimoire of the Thorn-Blooded Witch.* Weiser, 2014.
Lady Charlotte Guest, trans. *The Mabinogion.* 1877.
Hooke, Della. *Trees in Anglo-Saxon England.* Boydell, 2010.
Hughes, Kristoffer. *Cerridwen: Celtic Goddess of Inspiration.* Llewellyn Publications, 2021.

Hughes, Nathaniel, and Fiona Owen. *Intuitive Herbalism.* Quintessence, 2019.

Hutton, Ronald. *Blood and Mistletoe: The History of the Druids in Britain.* Yale University Press, 2009.

Jones, Mary, trans. The Cattle-Raid of Regamna, The Yellow Book of Lecan, the Táin Bó Cúailnge. https://www.maryjones.us/ctexts/index_irish.html.

Kindred, Glennie. *Earth Wisdom: A Heartwarming Mixture of the Spiritual, the Practical and the Proactive.* Hay House, 2011.

Kindred, Glennie. *Walking with Trees.* Permanent Publications, 2019.

Leahy, Arthur Herbert, trans. *Romances of Ireland, Vol. I.* Ballantyne, 1906.

Laurie, Erynn Rowan, trans. *The Cauldron of Poesy* as featured in *The Druid's Primer* by Eastwood, L. Moon Books 2012.

Lévy-Bruhl, Lucien. *L'Experience Mystique et Les Symboles Chez les Primitifs.* Librarie Felix Alcan, 1938.

Lucius Annaeus Seneca. *Moral Epistles,* vol. I. Translated by Richard M. Gummere. The Loeb Classical Library. Harvard University Press, 1917–25.

MacCulloch, John Arnott. *Celtic Mythology.* Dover, 2004.

MacLeod, Sharon Paice. *Celtic Cosmology and the Otherworld.* McFarland, 2008.

Mac Mathúna, Liam. "Irish Perceptions of the Cosmos," *Celtica* 23 (1999): 174–175.

Manco, Jean. *Blood of the Celts: The New Ancestral Story.* Thames & Hudson, 2015.

Meyer, Kuno, trans. "The Wooing of Emer." *Archaeological Review* 1 (1888), via Rosalind Clark, "Aspects of the Morrígan in Early Irish Literature." *Irish University Review* 17, no. 2 (Autumn 1987).

Morpheus, Ravenna. *The Book of the Great Queen.* Concrescent, 2015.

Nagy, Joseph Falaky. "Orality in Medieval Irish Narrative: An Overview." *Oral Tradition* 1/2 (1986): 272–301.

O'Rahilly, Cecile, ed. *Táin Bó Cúalnge from the Book of Leinster.* Dublin Institute for Advanced Studies, 1967.

Orr, Emma Restall. *The Wakeful World: Animism, Mind, and the Self in Nature.* Moon Books, 2012.

Plato. *The Republic of Plato, The Ten Books, Complete and Unabridged.* Penguin Classics of Greek Philosophy, 2021.

Plato. *Phaedrus.* Penguin Classics, 2005.

Rankine, David, and Sorita D'Este. *The Guises of the Morrigan.* Avalonia, 2005.

Shaw, John. "A Gaelic Eschatological Folktale, Celtic Cosmology, and Dumézil's 'Three Realms.'" *Journal of Indo-European Studies* 35 (2007): 250.

Schulke, Daniel, A. *Veneficium: Magic, Witchcraft and the Poison Path.* Three Hands, 2018.

Taplin, Kim. *Tongues in Trees: Studies in Literature and Ecology.* Green Books, 1989.

Three Initiates. *The Kybalion, Hermetic Philosophy.* St. Martin's Essentials, 2020).

Weber, Courtney. *The Morrigan: Celtic Goddess of Magic and Might.* Weiser, 2019.

Wilby, Emma. *Cunning Folk and Familiar Spirits.* Sussex Academic Press, 2005.

ABOUT THE AUTHOR

Joey Morris is a priestess of the Morrigan and a hedge witch who has been on the path of Celtic witchcraft for over twenty-five years. She specializes in spirit work, shadow work, and healing. Joey runs the popular Starry Eyed Witch YouTube channel, which boasts over 17,000 subscribers, as well as her own blog and witch supply store, Starry Eyed Supplies. She lives in Plymouth, England. Find her at *www.starryeyedsupplies.com*.

TO OUR READERS

Weiser Books, an imprint of Red Wheel/Weiser, publishes books across the entire spectrum of occult, esoteric, speculative, and New Age subjects. Our mission is to publish quality books that will make a difference in people's lives without advocating any one particular path or field of study. We value the integrity, originality, and depth of knowledge of our authors.

Our readers are our most important resource, and we appreciate your input, suggestions, and ideas about what you would like to see published.

Visit our website at *www.redwheelweiser.com*, where you can learn about our upcoming books and free downloads, and also find links to sign up for our newsletter and exclusive offers.

You can also contact us at *info@rwwbooks.com* or at

Red Wheel/Weiser, LLC
65 Parker Street, Suite 7
Newburyport, MA 01950